## SO YOU'VE BEEN BITTEN BY A
# RADIOACTIVE SPIDER

## HOW TO SURVIVE THE MARVEL UNIVERSE

BY DANIEL KIBBLESMITH
ILLUSTRATIONS BY KYLE HILTON

**CHRONICLE BOOKS**
SAN FRANCISCO

All rights reserved. Used Under Authorization. No part of this book may be reproduced in any form without written permission from the publisher.

Library of Congress Cataloging-in-Publication Data

Names: Kibblesmith, Daniel, 1983- author | Hilton, Kyle illustrator
Title: Marvel so you've been bitten by a radioactive spider : how to survive the marvel universe / by Daniel Kibblesmith ; illustration by Kyle Hilton.
Description: San Francisco : Chronicle Books, 2025.
Identifiers: LCCN 2025020861 | ISBN 9781797233543 hardcover
Subjects: LCSH: Marvel Comics Group--Miscellanea | Comic books, strips, etc.--United States--Miscellanea | Comic strip characters
Classification: LCC PN6725 .K53 2025 | DDC 741.5/973--dc23/eng/20250514
LC record available at https://lccn.loc.gov/2025020861

Manufactured in China.

Design by Barbara Bersche.

For MARVEL
Jeff Youngquist, VP, Production and Special Projects
Sarah Singer, Editor, Special Projects
Jeremy West, Manager, Licensed Publishing
Sven Larsen, VP, Licensed Publishing
David Gabriel, VP, Print & Digital Publishing
C.B. Cebulski, Editor in Chief

10 9 8 7 6 5 4 3 2 1

Chronicle Books LLC
680 Second Street
San Francisco, California 94107
www.chroniclebooks.com

© 2025 MARVEL

# CONTENTS

- 8 INTRODUCTION
- 11 HOW TO USE THIS BOOK

## PART ONE: GETTING POWERS

- 14 SO YOU'VE BEEN BITTEN BY A RADIOACTIVE SPIDER
- 21 SO YOU'RE A MUTANT
- 30 SO YOU'VE SURVIVED A GAMMA BOMB
- 36 SO YOU'VE BEEN BOMBARDED BY COSMIC RAYS
- 41 SO YOU'VE BEEN GIVEN SUPER-SOLDIER SERUM
- 46 SO YOU'RE HOSTING THE PHOENIX FORCE
- 50 SO YOU'RE FLYING IN IRON MAN ARMOR
- 57 SO YOU'VE BONDED WITH A SYMBIOTE
- 61 SO YOU'RE THE ONLY ONE WITHOUT POWERS (A PEP TALK)
- 63 SO YOU NEED A SUPER HERO NAME

## PART TWO: CRISIS

- 68   SO GALACTUS HAS ARRIVED
- 74   SO THE HULK IS HULKING OUT
- 80   SO YOU'RE LOST IN THE MULTIVERSE
- 89   SO YOU'RE IN THE QUANTUM REALM
- 95   SO WHO YOU GONNA CALL? THE RIGHT HEROES FOR THE CRISIS
- 98   SO YOU'RE DEALING WITH MAGIC
- 108   SO YOU'RE FACING A DOOMBOT

## PART THREE: DAY-TO-DAY

- 116   SO YOUR CAT IS A FLERKEN
- 120   SO YOU THINK YOU'VE FOUND A SKRULL
- 124   SO YOUR JOB MAY BE A FRONT FOR HYDRA
- 128   SO YOU NEED TO LIFT THOR'S HAMMER
- 137   SO YOU'VE GOT LEGAL TROUBLE
- 142   SO YOU NEED TO SPEAK GROOT

## CONCLUSION

- 146   SO YOU'VE FINISHED THIS BOOK

- 148   ACKNOWLEDGMENTS
- 148   ABOUT THE AUTHOR
- 148   ABOUT THE ILLUSTRATOR

# INTRODUCTION

> "WELCOME TO THE X-MEN, KITTY PRYDE.
> HOPE YOU SURVIVE THE EXPERIENCE!"
> – COVER BLURB, *THE UNCANNY X-MEN*, VOL. 1, #139

Welcome to **Earth-616**. Maybe you've lived here your entire life. Or perhaps this is your first visit—what the locals call a *Journey Into Mystery*. Either way, your life is about to change forever.

Earth-616 is a world of amazing and spectacular people and sights—but don't let the "Earth" part fool you. The universe is just that: *an entire universe*, extending into the cosmic depths of space and the magical realms beyond our reality.

What makes this universe truly special is that it's populated not only with heroes, villains, gods, and monsters, but also with everyday citizens who live alongside all these marvels. This world is full of people just like you who spend their days going to work, raising families, and grocery shopping—all the while hoping that the Incredible Hulk doesn't throw a car into the produce section.

But most excitingly, many heroes of Reality-616 *began* their legends as ordinary people. Sure, some were born into royalty and godhood, but most were just regular folks in the right place at the right time to be bitten by a radioactive spider, to get zapped by cosmic rays, to discover their hidden mutant power, or to find themselves flying above the city in a high-tech suit of armor. It can happen to anyone. It can happen to YOU.

And after having their lives transformed by miraculous circumstances, every one of these people asked themselves the same question: "Now what?" That's where this book comes in.

*So You've Been Bitten by a Radioactive Spider* is your guide to the Marvel Universe and your new place in it. From learning how your powers work to choosing a super hero name to spotting shape-shifting aliens, this book contains all the knowledge you need to begin your own uncanny origin story and first astonishing adventure. It will teach you the skills to stay alive through weekly apocalypses and cosmic crises. It's a marvelous universe, but it's also a dangerous one. This book will help you survive the experience.

So read on, true believer. Your legend begins now.

# *HOW TO USE THIS BOOK*

This book is a comprehensive, but also individualized, orientation guide to the Marvel Universe. If you are facing a particular dilemma—for example, how to lift Thor's hammer—turn directly to that chapter. Otherwise, this book may be read straight through or browsed in any order to fully prepare you for all adventures to come.

Watch for boxes like these to receive topical tips from some of Marvel's greatest heroes themselves:

> **FANTASTIC FACT!**
>
> *General knowledge and trivia from the infinitely elastic brain of Mister Fantastic.*

> **TONY'S TECH TIP!**
>
> *Technology, math, and engineering advice for those (like Iron Man) who rely on brains and gear more than super powers.*

> **USE YOUR SPIDER-SENSE!**
>
> *No one knows the danger ahead better than Spider-Man. Use these tips to stay one leap ahead of danger.*

# PART ONE

# *GETTING POWERS*

# SO YOU'VE BEEN BITTEN BY A RADIOACTIVE SPIDER

> "CHANGE ALWAYS COMES.
> WHAT MATTERS IS HOW YOU FACE IT."
> – MILES MORALES, *MILES MORALES: SPIDER-MAN*, VOL. 1, #29

It's more common than you think. There you are, enjoying a class trip to an atomic science lab or chilling on your uncle's couch when suddenly—CHOMP! You've been bitten by a radioactive (or genetically altered) spider. It can happen to anyone (see Fantastic Fact! on page 20). This chapter will cover the basics of radioactivity, common spider-person abilities, and how to navigate your new great powers and responsibilities.

## WHAT IS RADIOACTIVITY?

The Multiverse is positively radiating with different types of radioactivity, but this is the baseline model. Simply put, radioactivity is energy released by certain types of atoms during the decaying of their nuclei—including uranium, radium, and plutonium. But forget what you think you know about this deadly, invisible force of nature. In the Marvel Universe, radioactivity has one function: to give people super-powers.

> **EDITOR'S NOTE:** DO **NOT** EXPOSE YOURSELF TO RADIOACTIVITY IN ANY NON-COMIC BOOK UNIVERSE.

## WHAT TO EXPECT

After the initial sting of the spider's bite, there will be a burning sensation around the puncture, followed by symptoms like fever, chills, dizziness, and finally—unconsciousness.

> **USE YOUR SPIDER-SENSE!**
>
> *If you want to keep your transformation a secret, lock your door. It's pretty common for newly powered Spider-Folk to wake up on the ceiling.*

## YOUR NEW POWERS

The bite of a radioactive spider will transfer biological traits from the spider to yourself, which may include:

- ADHERING TO AND CRAWLING UP WALLS
- ENHANCED STRENGTH ("the proportionate strength of a spider")
- ENHANCED AGILITY AND BALANCE
- A "SPIDER-SENSE" WARNING YOU OF DANGER JUST BEFORE IT OCCURS (which might've been useful *before* you were bitten by an irradiated arachnid)

## GENETICALLY ALTERED SPIDERS

This modern, more recent update to the traditional radioactive spider bite bestows identical abilities, as well as potential bonus powers:

- A BIOELECTRIC STING, OR VENOM BLAST, TO INCAPACITATE ENEMIES
- TEMPORARY INVISIBILITY
- COOLER SHOES

## SPIN A WEB, ANY SIZE?

Surprisingly, one spider-power you probably won't receive is the ability to organically generate spiderwebs—a must-have for web-swinging across town, tying up bad guys, or reaching the remote control without having to stand up. For your web-spinning needs, you'll need to use your genius-level science skills to build a pair of web-shooters for both wrists.

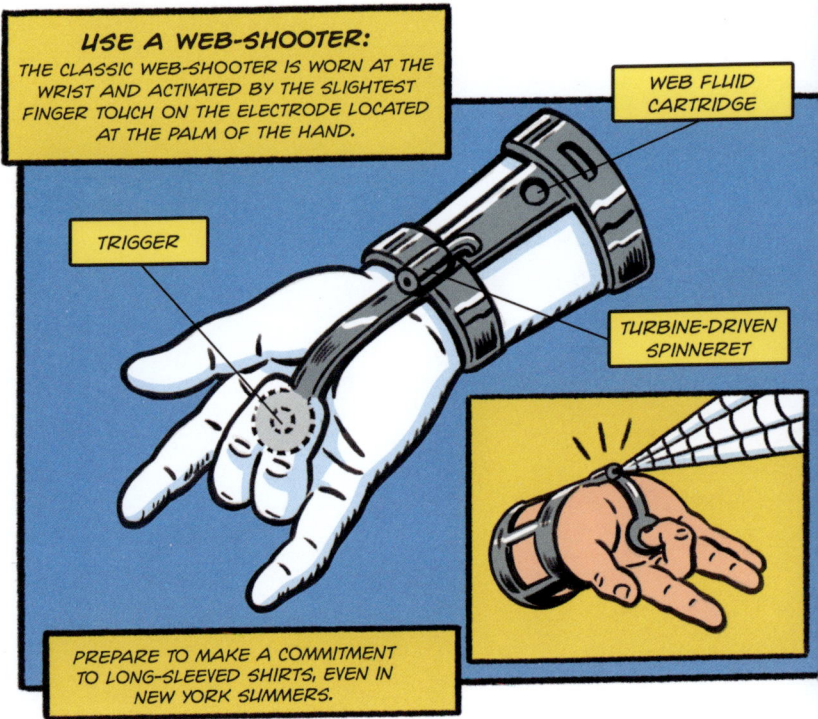

**USE A WEB-SHOOTER:**
THE CLASSIC WEB-SHOOTER IS WORN AT THE WRIST AND ACTIVATED BY THE SLIGHTEST FINGER TOUCH ON THE ELECTRODE LOCATED AT THE PALM OF THE HAND.

WEB FLUID CARTRIDGE

TRIGGER

TURBINE-DRIVEN SPINNERET

PREPARE TO MAKE A COMMITMENT TO LONG-SLEEVED SHIRTS, EVEN IN NEW YORK SUMMERS.

If science isn't your strong suit, remember: This is the Marvel universe. You can practically throw a rock and hit a scientist who can help you—assuming the scientist you threw a rock at doesn't get angry and turn into the Hulk.

> **TONY'S TECH TIP!**
>
> *Spider-Man's artificial webbing dissolves after about one hour, which is why you never see it hanging off buildings for long—and why you shouldn't trust any "collectible" examples that you find at auctions.*

## YOUR FIRST WALL-CRAWL

Powers are nothing without practice. Follow these climbing tips to start moving up in the world.

**1** ***Start with a Stretch:*** Experts recommend dynamic stretches before a climb—such as lunges and torso twists—and static stretches afterward, like holding a hamstring or quadricep stretch for as long as forty-five seconds. The warm-up will aid your agility and speed, while the cooldown will help prevent injuries. That is, injuries that don't involve getting electrocuted or swatted by a massive lizard tail.

**2** ***Lift with Your Legs:*** You may have the proportional strength of a spider, but *all* your muscles grew proportionately—which means your legs are still stronger than your arms. Pushing from below, rather than pulling from above, will help you spring upward faster and conserve upper-body strength, which you may

**FOLLOW WALL-CRAWLING 101:** START WITH A STRETCH. FOR STABILITY, KEEP MULTIPLE POINTS OF CONTACT WITH THE WALL. WHEN MOVING UPWARD, USE THE STRENGTH IN YOUR LEGS.

**1. STRETCH**

**2. USE THE STRENGTH IN YOUR LEGS**

**3. MAINTAIN THREE POINTS OF CONTACT**

need later to lift an entire building in an unforgettable triumph of heroic spirit.[1]

**❸** *Maintain Three Points of Contact:* Whether climbing a ladder or scaling the Empire State Building, stability is key. Maintain three points of contact with your climbing surface at all times—either two feet and one hand, or one foot and two hands. One exception to this rule is *vertical running*, i.e., sprinting up the side of a building, which should only be attempted in extreme emergencies, such as chasing a Goblin Glider or being late for work.

## YOUR NEW RESPONSIBILITIES

Spider-powers are not all fun and games. Your new life makes you a target for villains, especially those with their own animal motifs, like octopuses, vultures, rhinos, scorpions, lizards, chameleons, gibbons, jackals, kangaroos, black cats, white rabbits, and probably more by the time you read this. As a general rule, super villains are very unclear on which animals are the natural enemies of spiders. Their best guess? All of them.

From the moment you're bitten, your loved ones will be imperiled and your city will be in danger. It's up to you to make the sacrifices necessary to protect the people you care about. Oh—and if you have a beloved uncle you need to say anything important to, you might want to give him a call. Like, right now.

---

[1] Further reading: *Amazing Spider-Man*, Vol. 1, #33.

### FANTASTIC FACT!

*If you've spent much time in the Multiverse, you know we mean ANYONE. Spider-powers have been documented in:*

- 🕷 *COWBOYS (WEB-SLINGER)*
- 🕷 *CATS (SPIDER-CAT)*
- 🕷 *ELDERLY AUNTS (SPIDER-MA'AM)*
- 🕷 *CARTOON PIGS (SPIDER-HAM—technically a spider bitten by a radioactive pig)*
- 🕷 *DINOSAURS (SPIDER-REX)*
- 🕷 *VEHICLES (PETER PARKEDCAR)*

*If you can imagine it, a radioactive spider has probably bitten it.*

# SO YOU'RE A MUTANT

> "THIS IS MY POWER! MY MUTANT POWER!...READY OR NOT, HERE I COME!"
> – KATHERINE "KITTY" PRYDE, *CLASSIC X-MEN*, VOL. 1, #35

There's no such thing as "normal." Everyone is born with unique quirks that make us individuals. Maybe you can roll your tongue or wiggle your ears. Maybe your eyes project concussive beams that can flatten a house. If your personal quirk sounds more like that last one, congratulations/sorry—you may be a MUTANT.

There's a difficult path ahead of you. Some might even say this world "hates and fears" you. But it's still a world worth fighting for. Or, if you decide you're a so-called Evil Mutant, a world worth conquering. This chapter will help you navigate your newfound identity, powers, and the society that might not be ready to accept them.

## WHAT IS A MUTANT?

DNA (deoxyribonucleic acid) is a molecule in our cells composed of genes—individual sections of DNA that serve as the basic unit of hereditary information passed down from our parents. In the Marvel Universe, a mutant is a human born with the X-Gene, which unlocks superhuman abilities and, sometimes, physical transformations. The X-Gene can be passed down from mutant parents or occur spontaneously.

> **FANTASTIC FACT!**
>
> *The X-Gene may be the result of genetic tampering by Celestials—ancient, godlike beings who had a hand in creating early humanity. Evolution is real, but sometimes an alien the size of a skyscraper gives it a nudge.*

Mutantkind is also a culture unto itself, leading some mutants to refer to themselves not as humans at all but as a newly evolved species: *Homo superior*. This distinction can be useful for instilling fear and getting out of petty human obligations like coworker birthday parties and taxes.

Not all mutants are super heroes or super villains, but the ones that *do* engage in colorful, costumed combat tend to fall into two camps: Professor Charles Xavier's heroic X-Men and the Brotherhood of Evil Mutants, sometimes led by Xavier's best frenemy, Magneto. Over the years, however, these factions have blurred and overlapped, with heroes becoming villains, villains becoming heroes, dead heroes returning as alive villains, and all this taking place during frequent trips to outer space, lost dinosaur continents, sentient islands, and postapocalyptic futures.

Even for the Marvel Universe, your life just got complicated.

## HOW DO YOU KNOW IF YOU'RE A MUTANT?

The X-Gene typically activates during puberty, although some mutants might be active from birth—with adorable little baby wings, an adorable baby tail, or an adorable baby humanoid glob of pink protoplasm with visible skeleton. In adolescents, mutant powers usually manifest as an uncontrolled outburst during a moment of extreme stress. Which, for adolescents, is basically EVERY moment.

If you notice a sudden drop in temperature, a cacophony of voices in your head, or red-tinted vision and painful pressure behind your eyes, immediately ask your teacher for a bathroom break and make your way to the nearest parking lot or empty football field—anywhere that you're less likely to annihilate your hometown.

## POSSIBLE MUTANT POWERS

Mutant powers are the most varied and specific powers in the Marvel Universe. Some are less useful than others—*much* less. All the following are actual, documented mutant powers that you should be on the lookout for:

- READING MINDS
- CONTROLLING THE WEATHER
- INSTANTANEOUS HEALING
- WALKING THROUGH WALLS
- PREHENSILE TONGUE
- ACIDIC VOMIT
- EXTERNAL DIGESTIVE SYSTEM IN THE FORM OF TWO GIANT MAGGOTS
- GENERATING AND EJECTING GOLDEN SPHERES OUT OF YOUR BODY ("goldballs")
- TRANSFORMING YOUR BODY INTO ANY FLAVOR OF ICE CREAM
- *POOPING* ICE CREAM
- CLAWS (helpful for cutting hard-frozen ice cream)

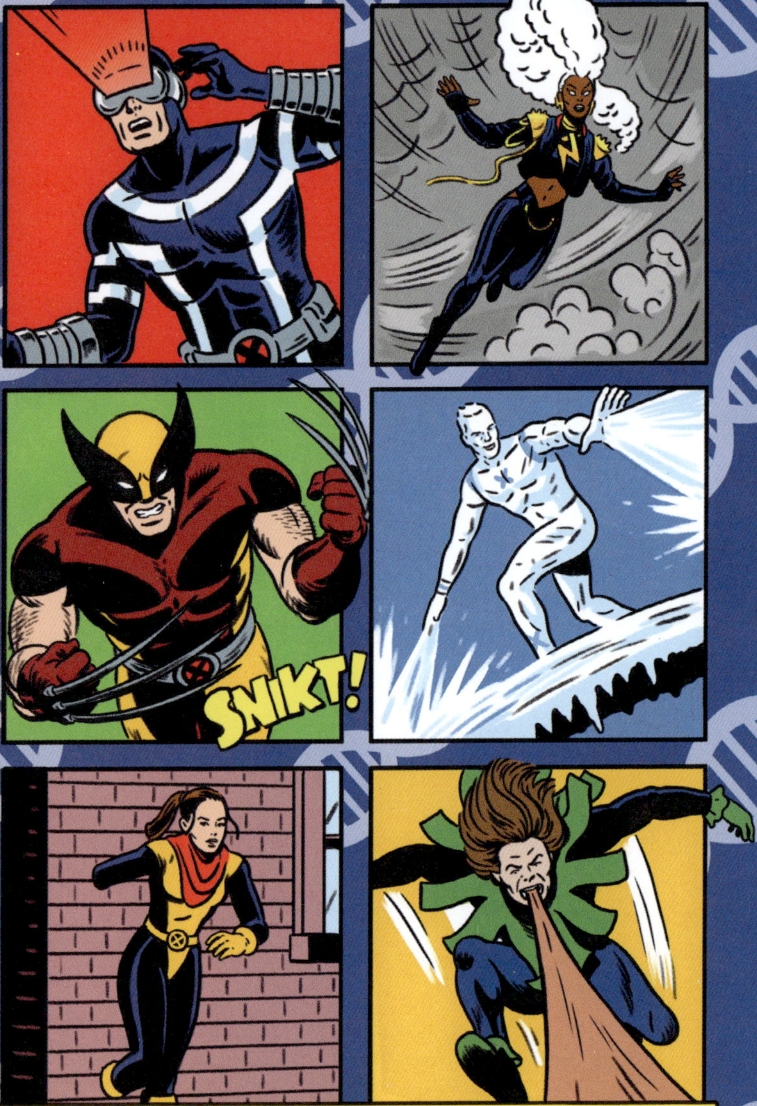
SNIKT!

**THIS IS YOUR POWER:** THE MUTANT POWERS GRANTED BY YOUR X-GENE ARE UNPREDICTABLE. LEARN AS MUCH AS YOU CAN ABOUT YOUR NEW ABILITIES AND YOU'LL FIND A WAY TO MAKE THEM USEFUL.

> **FANTASTIC FACT!**
>
> *Some mutants also evolve secondary mutations later in life, often as defense mechanisms. Documented secondary mutations include organic diamond form, organic ice form, or becoming a giant blue kitty in little glasses,[1] which will cause your enemies to let their guards down and take their phone cameras out.*

## OMEGA-LEVEL MUTANTS

Some mutants are deemed so powerful they receive the designation "Omega Level," meaning the limits of their power cannot be measured. Possible Omega-Level powers include magnetism, reality manipulation, weather manipulation, and in the case of the X-Man known as Gambit, Omega-Level abs.

## FOR OR AGAINST HUMANITY

In deciding whether to use your mutant abilities to fight for or against humanity, consider the following pros and cons of humans...

---

[1] Further reading: *New X-Men*, Vol. 1, #114.

| PROS | CONS |
|---|---|
| <ul><li>Invented movies</li><li>Capacity for reason</li><li>Cute babes</li><li>Creative spirit</li><li>Art and music</li><li>Ambition</li><li>David Bowie was a human!</li><li>For all their flaws, humans are ultimately a noble and caring race, taking their first baby steps on the evolutionary scale and aspiring to transcendent greatness that may one day reach the stars.</li></ul> | <ul><li>Talk in movie theaters</li><li>Fall for anything</li><li>Loaded diapers</li><li>AI-generated social media memes</li><li>Posers talking about art and music</li><li>Environmental destruction</li><li>Was he, though?</li><li>THEY TALK IN MOVIE THEATERS.</li></ul> |

---

**TONY'S TECH TIP!**

*X-Men founder Professor Xavier locates mutants using Cerebro, a computer-helmet combo that amplifies his psychic reach. Remember, spying on people is perfectly acceptable if it's for a good cause.*

## "MOM, DAD . . . I'M A MUTANT."

As most mutants discover their mutation around puberty, this typically means you're still living with parents and may have to have an awkward conversation about your new identity and/or leveling the garage when you sneeze. Here are some tips on how to safely and respectfully have "the big talk."

**WEIGH THE PROS AND CONS:** Being publicly known as a mutant may lift a weight off your shoulders—or put a target on your back. Take the temperature of your household by asking your parents for their opinions on mutant celebrities (like famous mutant musicians Dazzler and Lila Cheney, or fashion designer Jumbo Carnation). Weigh their reactions to these well-liked celebs against any recent *negative* mutant news like, say, Magneto turning the Brooklyn Bridge into galvanized-steel spaghetti.

**START SLOW AND SMALL:** Consider telling a few close friends before having any high-stakes family conversations. This will help you build an emotional support base—and if those friends are *also* mutants, it is shockingly easy for you to get your own X-Men spin-off team. You can probably apply via an app at this point.

**KNOW YOUR GOALS:** What change do you hope to bring about by having this conversation? There are any number of reasons to reveal you're a mutant: feeling more authentically like yourself, publicly participating in mutant culture, or letting your parents know you're enrolling in a boarding school that may or may not be a paramilitary organization with a stealth jet under the basketball court and a gymnasium that tries to hurt you.

**BE DIRECT:** Don't make a confusing situation more confusing. State your point clearly and briefly to the effect of "Mom, Dad, I'm a mutant." Once that's been established, *then* you can break out the PowerPoint that explains you're also technically the son of Mom's clone, raised in a dystopian future, where you also became a techno-organic virus–infected cyborg. Keep it simple to start.

**BE OPEN:** Once you've said your piece, create space for your parents to process in silence and/or ask any questions they might have, like "Is this why you have pterodactyl wings?" or "Couldn't you have been helping clean the gutters this whole time with your pterodactyl wings?"

**THERE'S NO TIMETABLE:** If you're not in a safe environment to be yourself, and you can continue passing for human, there's no pressure to reveal your powers at all. You can keep them a secret until adulthood and then do what most X-Men *and* twentysomething humans do: move to New York and begin making a lot of dramatic mistakes.

**HOW TO TALK TO YOUR PARENTS:** CHOOSE A COMFORTABLE CIRCUMSTANCE TO TALK TO YOUR PARENTS ABOUT YOUR NEWFOUND POWERS.

# *SO YOU'VE SURVIVED A GAMMA BOMB*

> "I'M THE NICE MONSTER."
> – RICK JONES, *HULK*, VOL. 2, #2

Duck and cover! If there's one job that's always hiring in the Marvel Universe, it's scientist—specifically, scientists who can build weapons.

When genius scientist Bruce Banner built an experimental gamma bomb, he didn't expect to take the brunt of it himself—shielding a young man who mistakenly rambled onto the testing site. The rest is history: You wouldn't like him when he's angry.

But just because you've been bombarded by gamma rays doesn't mean you have to be all green and grumpy about it. Hulks come in a rainbow of colors and personalities, and all shapes and sizes—well, typically one size: BIG. This chapter will help make sure your new dual life goes smashingly.

## WHAT ARE GAMMA RAYS?

Gamma rays are a form of electromagnetic radiation generated by expenditures of immense power. In space, they can be found in supernova explosions and around black holes. Here on Earth, they might be present in lightning strikes and nuclear detonations. All the usual places a future hero would normally hang out.

Gamma rays have so much penetrating power that they can only be stopped by several inches of dense material, like lead or concrete. This means that they can easily pass through the human body, like their less harmful cousin, X-rays.

> **FANTASTIC FACT!**
>
> *The Hulk also has a less harmful cousin.*

This exposure can damage tissue and DNA—or, here in the Marvel Universe, *alter* DNA, periodically shape-shifting you into a superstrong alter ego, usually triggered by anger or stress. Think Dr. Jekyll and Mr. Hyde—if Mr. Hyde could leap three miles and throw a tanker truck one-handed. This is not to be confused with the actual Marvel villain also named Mr. Hyde, although asking you not to be confused at this point might not be fair or realistic.

> **TONY'S TECH TIP!**
>
> *Despite their similarities, gamma rays typically create Hulks, while X-rays do not typically create X-Men.*

## KEEP YOUR COOL

Unlike most other super-types, many Hulks spend much of their time as their original, powerless selves. It's only when triggered that they "hulk out" and transform. Use these tips to keep calm in even the most stressful of circumstances:

- MEDITATION
- HERBAL TEA
- COZY MYSTERY PROGRAMS
- OKAY, THERE'S AN AD. We can just skip that. You can't skip the ad. *Why can't you skip the ad?! Why do pe*OPLE DO THIS? IT'S SO ANNOYIN— !!!!!!!!!!!!!!! !!!!!!!!?????

**KEEP YOUR COOL:** MAINTAIN A SENSE OF CALM AND "HULK OUT" ONLY WHEN YOU WANT TO.

## SHOPPING

"Hulking out" usually also means Hulking out of your outfit. To avoid purchasing a new wardrobe every time you lose your temper, look for oversized clothes in stretchy fabrics. Think ponchos, caftans, and wide-leg jeans. *Very* wide. Whatever you're picturing—wider.

> **USE YOUR SPIDER-SENSE!**
>
> *Just because you're a Hulk doesn't mean that you're invulnerable. Due to their destructive power, Hulks are often looked at as problems to be solved. In fact, Bruce Banner's best friends once shot him into space. He was pretty mad when he got back.*

## A RAINBOW OF HULKS

The most well-known Hulk is green, as is his cousin She-Hulk and many of his most famous foes. But green is just *one* color in the Hulk spectrum, and you may find yourself turning another shade of furious:

***CLASSIC GREEN:*** The madder they get, the stronger they get. A full dose of gamma radiation will typically render you a raging brute with a limited vocabulary, but a smaller dose (say, from a blood transfusion) sacrifices some of that strength for retaining verbal skills. Think less mass, more sass.

***RAGIN' RED:*** Red Hulks run hot, both in temper and temperature. The madder they get, the *hotter* they get, absorbing energy from their opponents and radiating it off their skin as extreme heat. And if you want to make one REALLY mad, crack an egg on them and take a video.

***GABBIN' GRAY:*** Bruce Banner's original Hulk form was gray, less strong, and more articulate—although still lacking Banner's highfalutin intelligence. Gray Hulks are working-class joes with street smarts, although somehow their "smart" decisions still seem to involve smashing.

***OSTENTATIOUS ORANGE:*** Rare, but it happens. Rather than being charged with gamma radiation, orange Hulks are *solar powered*. Ironically, this means Hulks have to "go green" to turn orange.

## HULKISMS

It's not rare for a Hulk transformation to slash your vocabulary, often down to third-person, two-word sentences. Memorizing these helpful phrases will allow you to continue holding totally normal conversations, seamlessly:

- HULK SMASH!
- HULK FRIEND.
- SMASH FRIEND!
- WHERE BATHROOM?
- ONE ADULT!
- HOW MUCH?
- MEDIUM RARE!
- THANK YOU!
- I'VE . . . I'VE DONE IT! *The formula worked! I'm as strong as the Hulk but with Banner's intellect! I've tamed the beast within! From this point forward, I shall no longer be the mindless, destructive brute who is a danger to friend and foe alike! I can speak! I can reason! I can—no, NO! I can feel the effects fading! I'm transforming back into a . . . a . . . !*
- HULK SMASH!

> ### TONY'S TECH TIP!
>
> *Through medical and psychological procedures, you may be able to achieve Smart Hulk—your original mind in your Hulk body. It's almost always a temporary state but perfect for Hulks who want to smash while having a philosophical debate about* why *they smash.*

# *SO YOU'VE BEEN BOMBARDED BY COSMIC RAYS*

> "I'M A SCIENTIST, SON; THERE'S NO SUCH THING AS WEIRD."
> – MISTER FANTASTIC, *FANTASTIC FOUR*, VOL. 4, #10

Space. In the Marvel Universe, it's not so much the "final frontier" as a frequent travel destination. Whether for work, pleasure, or against your will, you and everyone you know will likely be shot into space at some point. It can be a bumpy ride.

Should your experimental spacecraft encounter a storm of cosmic rays, you (and perhaps three of your passengers) will be transformed beyond your wildest dreams. Here's a helpful guide on what to do next.

## WHAT ARE COSMIC RAYS?

Cosmic "rays" are actually particles—the nuclei of former atoms that have been stripped of their electrons and blasted out into space at nearly the speed of light. Cosmic rays frequently bombard Earth, but they are harmlessly absorbed by our atmosphere. In space, however, special shielding is required to protect astronauts from exposure.

So if you leave Earth in a big hurry—say, in an experimental rocket—you might get a fantastically big dose of this potentially dangerous celestial radiation.

## YOUR NEW POWERS

Unlike gamma rays, which consistently push the average citizen toward a Hulkish direction, cosmic rays are more unpredictable. The most famous case of cosmic ray exposure in the Marvel Universe is, of course, the Fantastic Four—Earth-616's First Family of super hero adventurers. Using them as a starting point, you might acquire these powers:

***STRETCHING/PLASTICITY:*** Mister Fantastic (Reed Richards) has the power to stretch his limbs and contort his body into nearly any size and shape imaginable—be it a giant fist, a bouncing ball, or just changing a light bulb without a ladder.

*If you receive stretchy powers:* Invest in a wardrobe made of Richards's patented Unstable Molecules—clothing that stretches along with your body. If Unstable Molecules are unavailable, spandex is your friend.[1]

***INVISIBILITY AND FORCE FIELDS:*** The Invisible Woman (Susan Richards, née Storm) gained the ability to become invisible and subsequently discovered she could make other things invisible as well. She also developed the power to generate force fields of any shape and size, which were also invisible.

---

[1] See also "So You've Survived a Gamma Bomb."

**WORK TOGETHER:** THE VARIETY OF ABILITIES KNOWN TO COME FROM COSMIC RAY EXPOSURE CAN TOGETHER BECOME IMMENSELY POWERFUL WHEN YOU WORK AS A GROUP. DON'T NEGLECT THE ADJACENT POWER OF INDIVIDUAL CATCHPHRASES AND TEAM BRANDING.

***If you receive invisibility powers:*** Honor the heroism and integrity of the Invisible Woman by using your powers for good—and not going to the movies or riding airplanes for free.

**FIRE GENERATION, HEAT IMMUNITY, AND FLIGHT:** The Human Torch (Johnny Storm) returned to Earth and found his body ignited in flames. He soon discovered he could fly, project flames, and throw fireballs.

***If you receive fire powers:*** You now have incredible destructive power, the gift of flight, and the ability to go *supernova*—a massive detonation of your abilities that rivals the power of an exploding star. But forget all that; what you really need is a catchphrase. "Flame On," is already taken by the Human Torch, but you might consider: "Let's Heat Things Up!" or "It's Burnin' Time!" or even "Help, Help! I'm on Fire! Just Kidding. This Is on Purpose."

---

**FANTASTIC FACT!**

*A personal catchphrase can be legally trademarked if it is also used for commercial purposes, which Johnny Storm's almost certainly is. Remember to only buy officially licensed "Flame On!" merchandise from reputable vendors.*

---

**SUPERSTRENGTH AND ROCKY, INVULNERABLE SKIN:** The Thing (Benjamin J. Grimm) is a heroic but tragic figure. Although granted superstrength and invulnerability by cosmic rays, he is also forever trapped in a monstrous, rocklike body.

***If you transform into a superstrong rock creature:*** The urge to mourn your old life is understandable, but rather than falling into depression (as the Thing sometimes does), consider this: You are an awesome rock monster. Have you thought about cheering yourself up by tearing down a condemned building with a full-speed charge through the support beams?

---

### USE YOUR SPIDER-SENSE!

*Russian scientist the Red Ghost re-created the FF's transformation by venturing into space with his own foursome—himself, a gorilla, an orangutan, and a baboon. While they did all acquire powers, we strongly discourage locking yourself in a metal container with three panicking apes, much less shooting it into space.*

---

## FANTASTIC MARKETING

For various socioeconomic reasons, super-powered individuals in the Marvel Universe are not all treated with the same level of trust and excitement. To avoid raising fear and suspicion (e.g., "Mutants," "Spider-Man"), immediately rebrand yourself as FANTASTIC! You'd be surprised at what people just go along with.

# SO YOU'VE BEEN GIVEN SUPER-SOLDIER SERUM

> *"I'M LOYAL TO NOTHING, GENERAL—*
> *EXCEPT THE DREAM."*
> – CAPTAIN AMERICA, *DAREDEVIL*, VOL. 1, #233

Hot dogs. Apple pie. Punching evil dictators and celebrating with a hot dog and a piece of apple pie. Some values never change, almost like they've been frozen in ice. Steve Rogers and other patriots have taken on the mantle of Captain America to fight for justice and represent the best of who we can be. This metaphorical torch of liberty has been passed from generation to generation, from hero to hero. Now it's your turn.

Hold still. You might feel a slight pinch.

There we go. As the same Super-Soldier Serum that created Captain America begins coursing through your veins, here's how you too can become the guardian—and the symbol—your country needs right now.

## THE SUPER-SOLDIER SERUM

The original Super-Soldier Serum was invented during World War II by Dr. Abraham Erskine—a German scientist who defected to the United States to escape persecution for his Jewish heritage. The full formula was known only to Erskine and perfected for use on 4-F volunteer test subject Steve Rogers. Rogers was intended to be the first in an army of Super-Soldiers. But with Erskine's near-immediate assassination, the full formula was lost to history, and Steve Rogers became an army of one.

> **FANTASTIC FACT!**
>
> *While sometimes referred to as "The Last Good War," World War II did, in fact, also include some bad parts.*

Today, the phrase *Super-Soldier Serum* is shorthand for any number of attempts at re-creating Rogers's transformation. These are mostly multistage processes derived from what is known about the original experiment, often with painful and tragic results. But *you* will probably be fine.

## WHAT TO EXPECT

The transformation will dramatically affect your physique and abilities, making you stronger, faster, and likely even taller. For this reason, we suggest waiting until *after* the transformation to sign up for any dating apps.

BEFORE

AFTER

**PREPARE FOR YOUR DRAMATIC TRANSFORMATION:**
THE SERUM WILL MAKE YOU STRONGER,
FASTER, AND EVEN TALLER.

The serum is also known to increase mental efficiency, making it easier to learn, memorize, and strategize. Which means you'll have your choice of careers if, for some reason, you don't want one that involves being shot at. Which brings us to—

VINTAGE MEDIEVAL

CLASSIC ROUND

ENERGY SHIELD

**CHOOSE YOUR SHIELD:**
YOU'RE STRONG BUT NOT INVINCIBLE. PICK THE INDESTRUCTIBLE SHIELD THAT FITS YOUR STYLE.

**CLASSIC ROUND:** This is the gold standard—or more accurately, vibranium-iron alloy standard. Iconic, nigh unbreakable and equipped with offensive capabilities when thrown like a discus. Returns like a charm with practice. Okay, A LOT of practice.

**VINTAGE MEDIEVAL:** A design that has withstood the test of time. This was the make and model of the first Captain America shield, providing full coverage and coming to a sharp edge for hand-to-hand strikes. The perfect shield for owners of typewriters who still buy vinyl.

**ENERGY SHIELD:** It's not the 1940s anymore—let's get extreme. This wearable device generates a force field capable of everything Cap's classic shield does but without taking up space in your luggage. It is made of S.H.I.E.L.D.'s proprietary ultra-cooled plasma, and you might also consider upgrading to a flexible containment matrix that can take the shape of additional preprogrammed weapons, such as a sword or whip. Only for those with a Stark-level budget.

---

### USE YOUR SPIDER-SENSE!

*You will likely be called upon to become a symbol for your nation's ideals. Unfortunately, these can vary WILDLY depending on who is in charge at any given moment. Always remember to use your powers for what you know to be right rather than what others tell you is "right." When all else fails, do what the original Captain America did: Quit all the time to ride motorcycles across the country for a while.*

# SO YOU'RE HOSTING THE PHOENIX FORCE

> "YOU'RE JUST A MAN.
> I'M PHOENIX."
> – PHOENIX, *ASTONISHING X-MEN*, VOL. 1, #14

It's been said (a lot) that with great power there must also come great responsibility. But how do you behave responsibly with a power so great that it might be controlling *you*? Behold: the Phoenix Force—a cosmic entity older than the universe itself. The Phoenix Force is the fiery embodiment of destruction and rebirth, a being so incomprehensible that it cannot be described. But if you had to try, you might go with "giant flaming space bird." The Phoenix has chosen many human hosts to wield its terrible power over the eons. The most famous of these hosts is Jean Grey of the X-Men. The latest—is you.

## WHAT TO EXPECT

In a word: *power*. In two words: *It's complicated*. Jean Grey first attracted the attention of the Phoenix when she sacrificed herself to steer a crashing space shuttle into the water to save the lives of her fellow X-Men on board. The Phoenix then bonded with

Jean, resurrecting her, and she burst forth with a new costume and a new name—wait for it—Phoenix.

Following some outer-space adventures, including Jean destroying an entire planet (see "Going Dark" on page 48), it was discovered that the Phoenix who emerged from the water had not been Jean at all but actually a *copy* created and inhabited by the Phoenix Force while the *real* Jean healed from her injuries inside a cocoon at the bottom of New York City's Jamaica Bay.

Then, even later, the Phoenix Force returned to merge the original Jean Grey's memories with those of the Phoenix-created copy *and* a different Jean Grey clone who had emerged in the intervening time. What we're trying to say is—clear your calendar.

> **FANTASTIC FACT!**
>
> *It was recently discovered that the Phoenix Force can be divided among multiple hosts, as in the case of the Phoenix Five—a group of X-Men who responsibly shared the Phoenix's power, ensuring that it would take five times longer for them all to go completely bananas.*

## YOUR NEW POWERS

As the Phoenix, you now effectively exist beyond space and time. You are the universal nexus of psionic energy, and your powers are limited only by your imagination—but with special emphasis on psychic abilities:

- **TELEPATHY** (reading minds)
- **TELEKINESIS** (moving things with your mind)
- **EMPATHY** (sharing feelings with other minds)
- **PYROKINESIS** (creating fire with your mind)
- **CALCULATING THE TIP** (in your mind)

> ### TONY'S TECH TIP!
>
> *You can quickly calculate a 20% tip by rounding up, doubling the total, and moving the decimal point one place to the left. This is less of a tech tip and more of a math tip, or—wait for it—a tip tip.*

## GOING DARK

They say absolute power corrupts absolutely, and the Phoenix proves it again and again. "Bonding" inevitably leads to something more akin to full possession. Your biggest danger as a Phoenix host will be "going dark," or becoming irrational, vengeful, and capable of anything. Make an appointment with your local Xavier-level telepath to separate yourself from the Phoenix Force if you begin experiencing any of the following symptoms:

- **HALLUCINATING AN IMAGINARY LIFE IN THE VICTORIAN ERA**
- **JOINING A REAL, BUT ALSO VICTORIAN, EVIL SOCIAL CLUB AND/OR LARPING COMMUNITY**
- **DESTROYING ENTIRE PLANETS**
- **GREEN WARDROBE TURNING RED**

**RISE AND SHINE:** AS THE PHOENIX, YOU EFFECTIVELY EXIST BEYOND SPACE AND TIME. YOU ARE THE UNIVERSAL NEXUS OF PSIONIC ENERGY. TRY NOT TO BURN OUT.

## GOOD NEWS AND BAD NEWS

The Phoenix is a creature born of fire, and her hosts invariably burn out—both mentally and physically. Hosting the Phoenix—a symbol of destruction and rebirth—will most likely kill you, resurrect you, and repeat.

Goodbye. See you soon.

# SO YOU'RE FLYING IN IRON MAN ARMOR

> "I WON'T RUST IF YOU WON'T."
> - JAMES RHODES, *IRON MAN*, VOL. 1, #185

You don't need super-powers to be a super hero. Being a multi-billionaire, genius-level engineer will do just as well. When industrialist weapons designer Tony Stark was taken prisoner in a war-torn nation, he did what he'd done his entire life: He built his way out. Since Stark designed the first Iron Man suit, many heroes have worn the iconic armor, or their own custom variation. Now it's your turn. This chapter will teach you how to take flight—and how not to crash and burn.

## ARMOR UP

You need to know what you're getting into—literally. There have been many, *many* Iron Man suits over the years, along with countless variations worn by Stark's allies and enemies. Broadly speaking, the Iron Man armor is a heavily armed exoskeleton with capabilities including, but *absolutely not limited to*, the following:

- FLIGHT
- SUPERSTRENGTH
- REPULSOR RAYS (see below: "Repulsor Rays")
- COMMUNICATIONS ARRAY
- SELF-CONTAINED PERSONAL ENVIRONMENT
  (for use underwater and, with minimal upgrade, in space)
- SASSY ONBOARD COMPUTER PAL

## REPULSOR RAYS

This invention is the cornerstone of Tony Stark's Iron Man project. Simply put, repulsor rays are just that—rays that repulse. In some models, repulsor rays are described as beams of muons (think much heavier electrons) so dense that they hit their target with minimal heat but considerable concussive force of matter. It's like getting knocked across the room by a *really* powerful flashlight.

Jet boosters in the boots may seem like the obvious secret to Iron Man's flight, but because repulsor rays act as a counterforce, *re*pelling rather than *pro*pelling, they are the crucial complementary mechanism that allows for in-flight stability. Jet boosters are the gas. Repulsor rays are the brakes, the steering wheel, and the baseball bat in the trunk.

## FLYING BASICS

The Iron Man suit is operated via two complementary interfaces:

***NEURAL UPLINK:*** For split-second movements and common functions (thrusters and light weaponry)

***VOICE COMMAND:*** For complex analysis, real-time damage reports, and activating playlists

While repulsors are necessary for balance, hovering, and hard stops, the neural uplink also translates your brain's commands to your body into real-time flight instructions, instinctively activating the vast array of miniature boosters and rudders that allow for in-flight ascent, descent, and quick turns. Like riding a bike, but the bike costs multiple billions of dollars and you're not forced to enjoy fresh air and exercise.

Conventional pilots learn to master the **FOUR FORCES OF FLIGHT**:

- *Lift:* Manipulating air pressure using wings and propellers to get free boosts upward without expending energy.
- *Drag:* Wind resistance—the pressure of whatever you're flying into, depending on conditions and speed.
- *Weight:* Planes are heavy.
- *Thrust:* The force generated by the engines that drive you forward.

> **TONY'S TECH TIP!**
>
> *Of these forces, the Iron Man suit has to consider drag, weight, and thrust but not lift. Mostly because, with rare exceptions, I look stupid wearing wings.*

THWOOM

**MASTER FLIGHT BASICS:**
USE YOUR REPULSORS FOR BALANCE, HOVERING, AND HARD STOPS.

## YOUR FIRST FLIGHT

1. **Plant your boots** firmly on the ground with your arms lowered at your sides—palms open and also facing the ground.
2. **Activate repulsors** in flight mode rather than weapons mode. You want to hover, not blast two holes to Australia.
3. **Activate thrusters** at 20%—this, balanced by the repulsor rays, should achieve a sustainable hover.
4. **Pose for pictures**.
5. **Increase thrusters** slowly, by 10% at a time, up to 100% and try not to hit any birds.

## STICKING THE LANDING

Pilots, super hero and otherwise, keep in mind the rule of three, or the 3:1 rule of descent. To avoid going too down, too fast, allot yourself 3 nautical miles of forward motion for every 1,000 feet you need to descend—hence "three-to-one."

This rule does not strictly apply to the Iron Man armor, as it is equipped for precise vertical takeoff and landing, and can even use its repulsor technology to "brake" midair, hover, and/or turn. Reduce repulsor output gradually for a slow, vertical descent, and keep your palms steadily facing downward to avoid any unintentional, but extremely cool, midair flipping.

## COMMON IRON MAN MODELS

Before you can suit up, you need to choose exactly which suit you'll be piloting. Here's a list of popular models to consider blasting off in:

### MODEL 1
The timeless original. Bulky and bucket-headed in gunmetal gray. This first suit helped Stark escape from his captors, but is primarily kept around for nostalgia.

### MODEL 1 MK III
Similar, but with a shiny gold finish. Building a suit while *not* being held hostage gave Stark time for much-needed upgrades, but the bulkiness remains.

### MODEL 2
Leaner, faster, and the first suit in classic red and gold. This color scheme would become synonymous with Iron Man—if there's one thing Stark does as well as engineering, it's branding.

### MODEL 7, STEALTH ARMOR
This all-black model with stealth capabilities is perfect if you don't want your enemies to see you coming. Which raises the question—when *would* you want your enemies to see you coming?

### MODELS 13, 31, 36, 52, AND 71—THE HULKBUSTER SERIES
These suits were specially designed for combat with the Hulk, and the number of them says a lot about how successful they were.

**COMMUNICATIONS ANTENNA ARRAY**

**MULTISPECTRAL CAMERA HOUSING**

**AUDIO PROCESSING UNIT**

**ENCRYPTED SAFETY SEAL**

**TRI-BEAM PLATE**

**REPULSOR COOLING EXHAUST**

**LEFT PALM REPULSOR UNIT**

**KNEE PLEATING**

**FOOT PLEATING**

**FOOT ALTITUDE SENSOR**

---

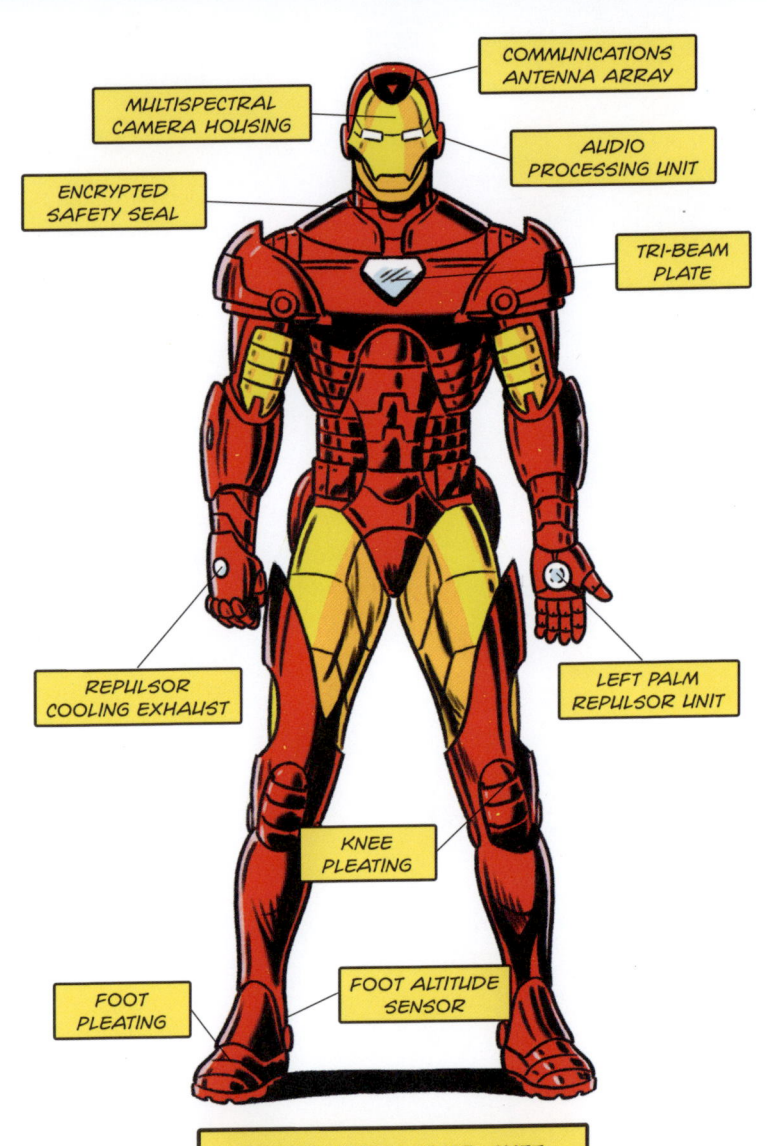

**GET TO KNOW YOUR SUIT:**
FAMILIARIZE YOURSELF WITH CRITICAL SYSTEMS AND COMPONENTS.

# SO YOU'VE BONDED WITH A SYMBIOTE

> "HI! WE'RE VENOM."
> – VENOM, *VENOM: LETHAL PROTECTOR* #1

Going to outer space is like the super hero version of jury duty—you can only put it off for so long. When Peter Parker's Spider-Man costume was damaged on an outer-space adventure, he luckily stumbled upon what he thought was a costume fabrication machine. If you think that sounds too weirdly convenient to be true, you're right. Spidey's snazzy new black costume turned out to be an alien symbiote with a mind of its own. This gooey black organism would become known as Venom, just one of the many, *many* alien symbiotes to take on human hosts. Most of them skew a little . . . murdery? Anyhow, good luck with this one.

## WHAT ARE SYMBIOTES?

In biology, a symbiotic relationship is one formed by two (or more) organisms that benefits both. Earthbound examples include the oxpecker, a small bird so named because it spends much of its time riding on—and pecking—the backs of four-legged African mammals, happily eating tiny, otherwise unreachable parasites. Both animals are healthier as a result of this partnership.

This is rarely the case with space symbiotes, which have less in common with the cute little bird and much, *much* more in common with the parasites.

In the Marvel Universe, *symbiote* is a shorthand, usually referring to protoplasmic organisms from the planet Klyntar, exiled from their hive-mind species for being "corrupted"—meaning prone to aggression and colonization, with some even infecting entire planets.

## SYMBIOSIS

When bonded with an average human, the symbiote will bestow powers including, but not limited to, the following:

- ENHANCED STRENGTH
- ARMOR/DURABILITY
- LIMITED SHAPE-SHIFTING ABILITY
  (may include forming claws or bladed weapons)
- CRAZY TEETH AND/OR A PREHENSILE TONGUE

---

### FANTASTIC FACT!

*There are multiple theories as to why symbiotes require a host at all, although they do feed on hormones secreted by human hosts, such as adrenaline and phenylethylamine—the latter being easily found in both chocolate and human brains. Many symbiotes just opt for both.*

## GETTING ALONG

A new roommate can get under your skin—especially when they're grafted to your skin. These conflict resolution strategies can help you learn to live with each other before someone gets killed.

- *Hold Honest and Open Discussions:* Periodically clearing the air will prevent minor resentments from building up into future arguments. Just because you're linked telepathically doesn't mean you can read each other's minds.

- *Don't Keep Score:* Avoid turning your homelife into a list of grievances by obsessing over who leaves dirty dishes in the sink more often or who keeps eating the neighborhood dogs.

- **Focus on "I" Statements Rather than "You" Statements:** This one might not apply, as most symbiote relationships are not an I and a You, but a *We*. Still, admitting that *we* always leave the toilet seat up is the first step toward change.

When all else fails . . .

## WEAKNESSES

Symbiotes are famously vulnerable to "sonics and fire." Sonics, meaning extremely loud noises or vibration-based weapons, and fire, meaning—fire. Spider-Man was first able to shed his symbiote by bringing himself deafeningly close to a church bell. You, too, can scare off your symbiote by bringing it someplace incredibly hot and unbearably loud. Like a teppanyaki restaurant

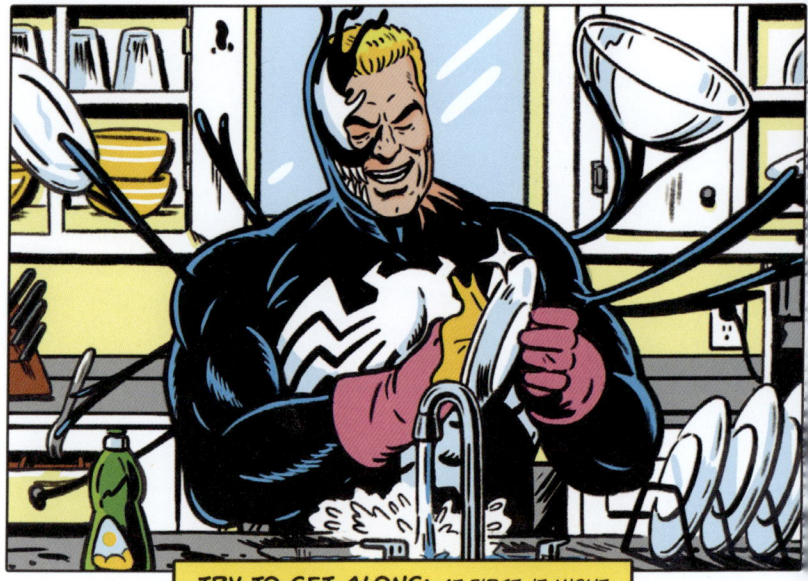

***TRY TO GET ALONG:*** AT FIRST, IT MIGHT FEEL UNCOMFORTABLE TO BE BONDED WITH A SYMBIOTE, BUT SOON YOU'LL FIND THERE'S NOTHING YOU CAN'T TACKLE TOGETHER.

### USE YOUR SPIDER-SENSE!

*The biggest danger of wearing a symbiote is the disappearance of your own identity. Remember, there is no "I" in Venom. Even when I was in Venom.*

# SO YOU'RE THE ONLY ONE WITHOUT POWERS (A PEP TALK)

> "I'M STRICTLY A
> BOW AND ARROW TYPE."
> – HAWKEYE, *IRON MAN*, VOL. 1, #196

Hey, champ. Let's talk for a sec.

We see you out there. You've got the look, the confidence, the skills. Maybe you're a gifted martial artist, an unnaturally talented marksman, or a world-class superspy. But at the end of the day, you don't have super-powers. And deep down, that stings like a Widow's Bite.

But you don't need powers to be a hero. Consider teachers, paramedics, firefighters, and the biggest heroes of all—people who buy books and comics at their local brick-and-mortar stores. Not all heroes wear capes. In fact, most of them don't. None of the Fantastic Four. Almost none of the X-Men. Only a few of the Avengers. It's a weird expression when you think about it.

Here's what you "bring to the table."

Every day is going to be a struggle. But don't let your old-fashioned, plain-vanilla human DNA dash your hopes of making

**BELIEVE IN YOURSELF:** YOU MAY NOT HAVE SUPER-POWERS, BUT YOU STILL HAVE A LOT TO BRING TO THE TEAM.

it to the big leagues. While the Asgardian gods and Wakandan royalty are up there slugging it out with the heralds of Galactus, that's when the bad guys in your own neighborhood think nobody is watching. The muggers, the gunrunners, and the people who *don't* patronize local bookstores. True sociopaths.

But they're wrong—somebody *is* watching. YOU. And every little bit helps. People will start to take notice, and pretty soon you'll be facing down an invading alien armada shoulder to shoulder with Asgardians and Hulks, telling them, "Don't worry, I've got this." And you know what? You *do.* We believe in you.

But for the love of god, get health insurance.

# SO YOU NEED A SUPER HERO NAME

> "I'LL NEED A NAME—WELL,
> GUESS SPIDERMAN IS AS GOOD AS ANY!"
> – PETER PARKER, *AMAZING FANTASY*, VOL. 1, #15

Some heroes are named at birth. Some by destiny. Others by the press or the adoring populace. Which is all very helpful, because the majority of heroes unexpectedly stumble into their powers and, therefore, have given *zero* thought to what their super hero name should be. After all, most people don't wake up in the morning planning on getting blasted by a Kree Psyche-Magnitron machine or receiving heightened senses from radioactive isotopes. And even if you *do* get super-senses, you might reject obvious choices like "Smell Man" or "Captain Hearing" and just name yourself after the devil for some reason. It's a personal decision—and a tough one.

| MODIFIER | NAME |
|---|---|
| 1 Black | 1 Knight |
| 2 Iron | 2 Raccoon |
| 3 Wonder | 3 Surfer |
| 4 Squirrel | 4 Duck |
| 5 Star | 5 Torch |
| 6 Grey | 6 Marvel |
| 7 Doctor | 7 Hulk |
| 8 Scarlet | 8 X |
| 9 War | 9 Fantastic |
| 10 Beta Ray | 10 Kid |
| 11 Two-Gun | 11 Bill |
| 12 Mister | 12 Machine |
| 13 Professor | 13 Witch |
| 14 She- | 14 Strange |
| 15 Ms. | 15 Queen |
| 16 The Human | 16 Lord |
| 17 Howard the | 17 Girl |
| 18 Silver | 18 Man |
| 19 Rocket | 19 Fist |
| 20 Moon | 20 Panther |

That's why we came up with a handy **SUPER HERO NAME GENERATOR TABLE**.

To find your new super hero name, just pick up a twenty-sided die (or use an online random number generator) and roll twice. The first result will assign you an adjective or modifier. The second number corresponds to your new proper name. Good luck!

**NOTE:** There are no rerolls. Your initial results stand. But don't worry, we promise that evildoers will cower in terror at the very mention of Doctor Bill, Squirrel Raccoon, or the Human Man. And if not "terror," certainly confusion that you can use to your advantage.

The only reroll exception occurs when your result is already the name of a famous Marvel hero. Trust us, you do not want that lawsuit.

# PART TWO

# *CRISIS*

# SO GALACTUS HAS ARRIVED

> "GALACTUS IS COMING. I HAVE HEARD THE LAMENTATIONS OF WORLDS—YET IF THERE ARE THREE MORE HORRIFYING WORDS IN ANY CORNER OF THE COSMOS, I'VE NOT HEARD THEM."
> – THOR, *THE MIGHTY THOR*, VOL. 2, #2

Panic.

Wait, wait, wait, wait—sorry! You're supposed to be a super hero. Now that you've got your super hero name and are fully oriented in your new powers (or powered suit), it's time to put them to use in the battle to save all humankind—yet again.

> **USE YOUR SPIDER-SENSE!**
>
> *But you should still probably panic.*

## WHO IS GALACTUS?

Galactus, the Devourer of Worlds, is an all-powerful cosmic being who survives by consuming the life force of planets and all who inhabit them. Once a mortal being called Galan of the planet Taa, Galactus is the sole survivor of a previous universe that preceded our own big bang. Granted immense power by that dying universe, he was transformed into an apocalyptic force of nature driven by one endless, aching thought: "I HUNGER." Galactus is neither good nor evil—he is inevitable.

> **FANTASTIC FACT!**
>
> *Intergalactic legend states that Galactus appears differently depending on the species of those observing him. To humans, he appears as a giant human. To a planet of sentient pizza slices— well, it would still make more sense to appear as a giant human, given that he's there to devour them.*

## THE POWER COSMIC

Not to be confused with cosmic rays (see "So You've Been Bombarded by Cosmic Rays"), the Power Cosmic is a nearly infinite cosmic power (hence the name) primarily associated with Galactus and his heralds. The Power Cosmic is most frequently used to fire projectile blasts and survive in the conditions of space, but its applications are almost without limit, including transmutation, teleportation (which makes a flying surfboard an interesting choice), and "hearing" the universe's electromagnetic fields—allowing heralds of a certain hungry immortal to sense where there might be sustenance.

## WHAT ARE HERALDS?

These are beings like the Silver Surfer—former mortals that the slow-moving Galactus has anointed and empowered to traverse the universe at superspeed, identifying planets worthy of consumption. As Galactus feeds faster than life can evolve and populate, his options for sustenance dwindle. As a result, Earth is consistently revisited, seemingly an irresistible target for his bottomless hunger. We're like the freshly baked chocolate chip cookie of inhabited worlds.

## WHAT ARE OUR OPTIONS?
Before you liquidate your savings and book that bucket-list skydiving trip, there's one proven strategy to slow the coming of Galactus and give you time to come up with a plan.

## TURNING A HERALD
This is surprisingly common. Upon his first visit, the initially brusque Silver Surfer came to appreciate Earth and its beauty—and one beauty in particular, the Thing's sometimes-girlfriend Alicia Masters. She sensed nobility in the Surfer and convinced him to betray Galactus—who punished him by exiling him to Earth, the planet he was so infatuated with. The Surfer quickly learned what we Earth locals already know: It has its downsides.

Another herald, Terrax, was chosen for his lack of morality, possibly to avoid another outbreak of sentimentality. This, too, backfired, as Terrax served Galactus out of fear rather than duty and overcame that fear often enough to betray him constantly.

Neither of these rebelling heralds were enough to stop Galactus on their own, but both made for uneasy allies, giving

**TURN THE HERALD:** THIS MAY NOT STOP GALACTUS BY ITSELF, BUT IT CAN SLOW HIM DOWN TO COME UP WITH A **REAL** PLAN.

the Fantastic Four (and others) enough time to come up with the *real* plan.

## HOW TO DEFEAT GALACTUS

You might have noticed that Earth is still here. To the all-powerful Galactus, humans are little more than ants. This analogy holds—we're stronger than we look, highly cooperative, and notoriously hard to get rid of. Here are some proven methods for defeating Galactus, pulled straight from the history of the Marvel Universe.

***NOTE:*** The following list might constitute spoilers if these were not, in fact, actual events that really happened.

***SCARED AWAY:*** The Fantastic Four's first face-off with Galactus ended when Mister Fantastic confronted Galactus with the Ultimate Nullifier—a weapon from Galactus's home planet, powerful enough to destroy Galactus along with the entire Earth and human race. Galactus agreed to spare Earth in exchange for the Nullifier's return, falling for Reed Richards's bluff of mutually assured destruction—assuming it was a bluff. In a crisis of that magnitude, even the smartest man in the world might be forced to do something cosmically reckless.

***DEFEATED BY THE POWER COSMIC:*** One of Galactus's aforementioned heralds was the Avenger Thor, who accepted the role and the tremendous power that came with it, promising to help Galactus defeat a cosmic mutual threat. Thor instead turned the Power Cosmic back on Galactus himself, temporarily killing him. You truly cannot find good help these days.

**CLOBBERIN' TIME:** Don't overthink it. Galactus might be an inevitable force of death, but at the end of the day, he's just a big, giant guy. In a later encounter with Galactus, who was weakened due to lack of sustenance, all the premiere heroes of the Marvel Universe—and Terrax—teamed up to beat the tar out of him in New York City. The final blow came when Mister Fantastic, using his own body as a slingshot, launched the rocky, superstrong hero the Thing directly into Galactus's face. Clobberin' David meets Space Goliath.

**DEFEATED BY GALILEO AND MICHELANGELO IN ANCIENT ROME:**
Before S.H.I.E.L.D., there was the Order of the Shield, an ancient secret society that included the most famous geniuses in all of history. Long story short, Galactus landed in Rome in 1502 and was blasted away by a clockwork machine built by Renaissance-era geniuses. Just like you learned about in high school.

**SMASHED BETWEEN TWO PLANETS:** This occurred in a fight with Thanos and did enough damage to force an injured Galactus into retreat. One drawback of this plan: Now you're fighting Thanos.

**"KILL" HIM WITH KINDNESS:** The butt-kicking, nut-eating hero known as Squirrel Girl quietly saved Earth from Galactus by greeting him with compassion; impressing him with her past defeat of their mutual enemy, Thanos (whom Galactus refers to as "a tool"); and steering Galactus toward a nut-filled planet to snack on instead of ours. There's a reason they call her "Unbeatable."

# SO THE HULK IS HULKING OUT

> "DON'T LOOK HIM IN THE EYE."
> – JACQUELINE MCGEE'S FATHER,
> *THE IMMORTAL HULK*, VOL. 1, #4

Death. Taxes. Hulk. Some things are unavoidable—and in the Marvel Universe, even *death* can be negotiable. But it's harder negotiating with a two-and-a-half-ton jade giant rampaging through your city. If you hear earthquaking foot stomps and someone roaring about "SMASHING" in the third person, consult this chapter immediately for how to make it through a "Hulk-out" in one piece.

## WHICH HULK IS IT?

For the purposes of this chapter, let's assume that the Hulk in question is an alter ego of mild-mannered scientist Bruce Banner—because it almost always is. Unfortunately, this still doesn't narrow it down. Not even counting the various She-Hulks and Red Hulks that populate his social circle, Banner alone has been host to many incarnations of the Hulk, each with their own strengths and weaknesses (but mostly strengths).

**SAVAGE HULK:** This is the most commonly seen Hulk and the one people are most likely to associate with the name "the Hulk." He's a bright-green, semi-articulate beast, overcome with rage but also claiming to simply want to be left alone. Our advice? Give him what he wants.

*Soothing techniques:* Savage Hulk can recognize and remember friends, including those from Banner's life, and has responded in the past to soothing pleas from people he trusts, usually a love interest or teenage sidekick. Unfortunately, the Hulk's enemies usually seize upon this moment of calm to start shooting at him again, restarting the entire cycle.

**GRAY HULK:** The first Hulk incarnation, this Hulk was gray rather than green, and the smallest of the Hulks—but also more articulate and cunning (see "So You've Survived a Gamma Bomb"). The transformation to Gray Hulk is typically triggered by sundown rather than a loss of temper, and he is reportedly strongest during a new moon and weakest when the moon is full. If Gray Hulk is wearing a suit (you heard us), this is the **Joe Fixit** incarnation—a Las Vegas–based enforcer for hire (you heard us again).

*Soothing techniques:* Gray Hulk is skeptical of humans but also arrogant, and can be reasoned with or flattered. Joe Fixit is also the only Hulk who can be appeased with a briefcase full of cash.

**SMART HULK (*"Professor Hulk"*):** This is either a "merged" Hulk, composed of Banner's personality in the Hulk's body, or a

**USE SOOTHING TECHNIQUES:** SAVAGE HULK CAN RECOGNIZE AND REMEMBER FRIENDS, AND BE CALMED BY PEOPLE HE TRUSTS. BUT IF HE DOESN'T RECOGNIZE YOU, *RUN.*

separate identity presenting Banner's "idealized" Hulk—as intelligent as Banner but free of his baggage and neuroses. And, like many middle-aged men, Banner thought the coolest version of himself would have a ponytail.

***Soothing techniques:*** Banner programmed himself with a subconscious fail-safe to prevent mindless Hulk-outs. If you make Professor Hulk angry enough to lose control, he instead turns back into Banner—sort of a *reverse* Hulk. Again, we suggest making fun of the ponytail.

**THE GREEN SCAR / WORLDBREAKER:** When a self-appointed "Illuminati" of the Marvel Universe's biggest brains shot their friend Banner into space, they were aiming for a lush, peaceful planet where the Hulk could happily retire. They missed. Who knew that geniuses with too much power could make mistakes? Landing on a world of gladiatorial combat, the Hulk evolved into the Green Scar persona in order to survive—as strong as Savage Hulk, as cunning as Gray Hulk, and as intelligent as Banner. The Worldbreaker persona was created as a result of the Hulk's newly adopted planet being destroyed, both enraging him and exposing him to the power of the planet's core. Worldbreaker Hulk returned to Earth to declare war, easily defeating Earth's mightiest heroes, gods, and monsters. The Worldbreaker was, by far, the strongest Hulk ever documented . . . until he wasn't.

***Soothing techniques:*** Surrender.

***IMMORTAL HULK:*** The worst of all possible worlds. Immortal Hulk was created as a result of the Hulk and Banner's many deaths and resurrections, coalescing as a monstrous persona also known as "Devil Hulk." This Hulk combines the strength of Savage Hulk, the cunning (and nocturnal schedule) of Gray Hulk, and raw power exceeding that of the Worldbreaker. Immortal Hulk does not want to be left alone. Immortal Hulk wants revenge.

***Soothing techniques:*** RUN.

## PLAN B

Let's assume soothing (or fleeing) the Hulk hasn't worked out, and you're not content to let him destroy the entire city. Here are some proven methods for defeating the Hulk that have worked in the past.

***HULKBUSTER ARMOR:*** The go-to move. Tony Stark is always tinkering with the latest version of the Hulkbuster Iron Man model (see "So You're Flying in Iron Man Armor"). This has mixed results, and the suits should be considered a very expensive one-time-use product.

***ADAMANTIUM:*** The unbreakable metal that coats the razor-sharp claws of the X-Men's Wolverine. In one of Wolverine's first high-profile throwdowns (before he revealed he'd been kicking around for a couple hundred years), Logan went one-on-one with the Hulk, and the two have been brawling ever since. Occasionally, Wolverine gets the upper hand, but the results are usually very, very bloody.

**THE POWER COSMIC:** Savage Hulk has gone toe to toe with the Silver Surfer a number of times and proven vulnerable to the Power Cosmic (see "So Galactus Has Arrived"). In one instance, the Surfer was even able to knock the Hulk down with a blow from his surfboard.

**HELLFIRE:** The fires of Hell (yes, that Hell) as projected by the flaming-skull-headed hero/antihero Ghost Rider have been shown to cause great pain to the Hulk, convincing him—at least in that moment—that he could be killed by them. This possibility has never been pursued, and Ghost Rider (and demons in general) can be as tricky to negotiate with as the Hulk, but the option theoretically remains.

**DIVINE LIGHTNING:** On the other side of the spiritual spectrum, divine lightning, as summoned by Thor, the God of Thunder, can briefly incapacitate the Hulk. This must be followed up with a *lot* of Thor-strength hammer blows. Even then, these two original Avengers are notoriously evenly matched in combat.

**NOTE:** If you do not possess any of the above, please reconsider that running plan we mentioned.

# SO YOU'RE LOST IN THE MULTIVERSE

> "I'M IN A PARALLEL UNIVERSE, FIGHTING AN ALTERNATE VERSION OF MYSELF ALONGSIDE A GROUP OF PARAHUMAN MERCENARIES WHO WANT ME TO HELP THE WRONGLY ACCUSED MAJESTRIX OF...DO YOU EVER GET HALFWAY THROUGH A SENTENCE AND FIND YOURSELF UNABLE TO BELIEVE THAT YOU'RE ACTUALLY SAYING IT?"
> – CAPTAIN BRITAIN, *THE DAREDEVILS*, VOL. 1, #8

By now, you know that the cosmic geography of the Multiverse is not limited to Earth and the alien planets that make up our universe but extends to countless universes existing alongside our own, separated by what all-seeing Uatu the Watcher calls "cosmic gossamer." Across this endless spectrum of universes, infinite possibilities are constantly unfolding, forcing us to ask the mind-bending question of "What if?" Ideas that we can barely fathom—like "What if Spider-Man was a cowboy?" or "What if Wolverine was even older?"—boggle the mind.

But unlike outer-space travel, where returning to Earth is as easy as turning the ship around 180 degrees and stepping on the gas, multiversal travel requires its own, much more esoteric means of conveyance. And with infinite destinations, getting back can be infinitely tricky. This chapter will cover the basics of the Multiverse, how to explore it, what to look out for, and (hopefully) how to get back home.

## **WHAT IS A MULTIVERSE?**

The "many-worlds interpretation" of quantum mechanics suggests that every possible outcome of a quantum measurement is manifested as reality in some "world." This theory is frequently explained using the famous thought exercise Schrödinger's cat—wherein a cat exposed to poison in a box can be considered both alive and dead until the box is opened and one outcome is confirmed. In any measurable scenario, if multiple outcomes are possible, the many-worlds theory suggests that, somewhere, *all* outcomes have spun off into their own realities. In the case of Schrödinger, this includes one universe where the cat is alive, one where the cat is dead, and two where everyone's mad that some guy is poisoning cats in boxes.

As with much of the science we have covered in this book, the Marvel Universe's version is more clear cut. Some universes are created by points of quantum divergence, where the potential for a different turn of events branches off into its own alternate history (e.g., "What if Gwen Stacy had lived?"). Other parallel universes simply *exist* without a clear point of divergence from any other known universe (e.g., "What if Spider-Man was a cartoon pig? That might be weird.").

In the multiversal organizational structure, the most familiar (or "prime") Marvel Universe is referred to as Earth-616. Many have been discovered, numbered, or otherwise named and cataloged, but infinitely more are yet to be explored—with new ones created every second.

## HOW DID YOU GET HERE?

Technically, you were already in the Multiverse, as it comprises all of space-time, but we get what you mean. There are any number of ways to traverse from one universe to another—from the mystical to the scientific to the superhuman. One quick disclaimer: Parallel universes differ in key ways from *dimensions*, *realms*, and nested *pocket universes* within our own. If that's too confusing to process, then you shouldn't have messed with any of the following:

***ARTIFICIAL INTER-UNIVERSAL PORTAL:*** An early technical solution to inter-universal travel was constructed by Reed Richards of the Fantastic Four—an artificial portal into what he then called "Sub-Space." This turned out to be an antimatter-based parallel dimension now referred to as the Negative Zone (see "So Which Universe/Reality/Etc. Are You in Now?").

***STAR-SHAPED PORTAL:*** The Marvel hero America Chavez has the ability to smash open star-shaped portals to other universes, punching and kicking holes in reality. Which, if you know her, is pretty on-brand.

***TALLUS:*** An amulet containing a shard of the M'kraan Crystal (see below: "Nexus(es) of All Realities"), the Tallus is the means of universe-hopping employed by the Exiles, a Marvel superteam that focused on multiversal heroics before it was cool.

***MAGIC:*** Via portals, astral projection, or just old-fashioned teleportation, sorcerers like Doctor Strange can mystically transport themselves to other realms. These realms may be "universes" like our own, or realms most easily described as various competing versions of Hell, or the mythic kingdoms where pantheons of famous gods dwell, or even the collective unconscious where dreams (and nightmares) are born.

***WEB WATCH:*** Also known as the Dimensional Travel Watch, but so nicknamed because it's the method of multiversal travel employed by the Web-Warriors—a team of alternate-universe Spider-Men, Spider-Women, Spider-Pigs, and Spider-Others.

## NEXUS(ES) OF ALL REALITIES

Believe it or not, you can also stumble into another dimension on foot. The Marvel Multiverse is home to the Nexus of All Realities, which is, by definition, more than one place—for multiple Nexuses of All Realities exist. These are places where universes overlap, and traveling from one to another can be so easy as to (frequently) happen by accident. Some of these nexuses include the following:

***MAN-THING'S SWAMP:*** The mysterious and mute swamp monster known as Man-Thing resides in a swamp in the

**SO YOU'RE LOST IN THE MULTIVERSE:** *DON'T PANIC! THE BEST WAY TO FIGURE OUT WHICH UNIVERSE YOU ARE IN IS TO STAY CALM AND OBSERVE YOUR SURROUNDINGS.*

Florida Everglades with an entry to the nexus at its center. This is the portal where the famous Howard the Duck, among others, was deposited in our universe by mysterious forces—leaving him "trapped in a world he never made." This is true of everybody, but Howard manages to complain about it more.

***THE M'KRAAN CRYSTAL:*** Older than known history, the M'Kraan Crystal is a reality-warping alien artifact that, while appearing small enough to sit on a table, contains a physics-defying city, a miniature sun / reality nexus, and access to the White Hot Room—the physical representation of the Phoenix Force's consciousness and the conceptual place where it incubates and resurrects itself. Shards of the Crystal can be used for multiversal travel, as in the construction of the Tallus.

***OTHERWORLD:*** A sort of Celtic-flavored Asgard, Otherworld is a multiversal nexus where Arthurian mythos is a reality. It is home to Camelot (in the province of Avalon) and historically was the home base for the many interdimensional incarnations of the hero Captain Britain.

---

### FANTASTIC FACT!

*The designation "Earth-616" comes from Otherworld, which is overseen by an Omniversal Majestrix who numbers and catalogs known universes. The argument for not numbering your own universe makes sense—you don't want countless billions of worlds arguing over who gets to be Earth-1. Personally, I think "Earth-4" has a nice ring to it.*

## SO WHICH UNIVERSE/REALITY/ETC. ARE YOU IN RIGHT NOW?

There are too many universes across the Multiverse to list, but some seem to attract more visitors than others:

If you see chunky-looking monsters and/or the polarization of your protons was reversed upon your arrival, you might be in the **Negative Zone**—an antimatter-based dimension beside our own (or possibly *within* our own; see "'Pocket' Dimensions" on the facing page). This is a harsh environment where life struggles to evolve, time passes more quickly, and alien warlords battle for supremacy—and to be the first to break out and conquer our world beyond.

If you see Mindless Ones—mute, golem-like brutes with glowing slits for eyes, you might be in the **Dark Dimension**. This is a Hell-like realm, most associated with frequent visitor Doctor Strange and ruled over by his demon nemesis, Dormammu.

If you see modern, stylish redesigns of familiar Marvel heroes, you might be in the **Reality-1610** (the "Ultimate Universe"). Recognizably similar, yet captivatingly different, iterations of the Ultimate Universe are triggered when seminal Marvel events occur *later* in a universe's life cycle. In other words, it's newer.

If everyone sounds like Shakespeare, you are in the universe of **1602**, so named because this is the year when super-powered humans began to emerge there. Consider it an Elizabethan-era Ultimate Universe. In other words, it's older.

If Wolverine looks old, even for him, this is the **Old Man Logan Universe** (not an *official* name but a helpful one). Adding to the confusion of multiversal travel, some possible futures accessible via *time-travel* within our *own* universe are also freestanding extant universes unto themselves. Aren't you glad you bought a guidebook?

> **USE YOUR SPIDER-SENSE!**
>
> *Between many, many clones and the multiversal counterparts, I've had a lot of experience fighting myself. Not to get too personal, but punching yourself in the face can be extremely therapeutic. Give it a try.*

## "POCKET" DIMENSIONS

In addition to parallel universes, the Multiverse also contains countless *pocket* dimensions—universes *within* universes (see "So Your Cat Is a Flerken"). Some are temporary, artificial constructs that serve as refuges or prisons. Others seemingly occur naturally, like the Negative Zone—which was described by one higher being as "a failed pocket universe resting inside an existing one . . . like a tumor."[1] A review almost savage enough for Yelp!

---

[1] Further reading: *Avengers*, Vol. 5, #21.

## HOW TO GET HOME

Easier said than done, but the answer is typically "the way you came." Whatever device or mystic portal you employed to leave your home universe should have recorded your origin point and have the power to return you there. The tricky part is that, if you've been whisked away to another dimension to begin with, it's usually to help eliminate a cosmic threat. Think of it like *The Wizard of Oz* rules—drop in randomly, explore a bizarre parallel world, and melt a villain. Getting home will take care of itself.

---

### FANTASTIC FACT!

*Not confused enough yet? Beyond the Multiverse there is an omniverse, which reportedly contains all multiverses, as well as mystic realms, afterlifes, fictional and story-based realities, and even competing universes with other famous super heroes that we probably shouldn't mention by name.*

# SO YOU'RE IN THE QUANTUM REALM

> "THE LAWS OF PHYSICS DON'T APPLY HERE. THE MICROVERSE REWRITES THE RULES."
>
> – THE WASP (NADIA VAN DYNE), *ANT-MAN & THE WASP*, VOL. 1, #1

The Marvel Universe extends in *all* directions: upward into the cosmos, sideways into parallel universes, and finally "downward" into *innerspace*—a mysterious Quantum Realm in which Marvel's shrinking heroes, like those who have taken on the mantles of Ant-Man and the Wasp, battle tiny tyrants in a microverse where the laws of physics break down and anything is possible. Especially if the "anything" is trying to kill you. If you want to stay alive down here, this chapter will help you start thinking small.

## WHAT IS THE QUANTUM REALM?

Let's start with something easy, like more quantum mechanics.

Quantum mechanics is the study of matter and energy at their most fundamental level—a field of research that attempts to understand nature at a scale smaller than that of atoms, where the rules of physics seemingly no longer apply. One famous example is the double-slit experiment, which helps illustrate the concept of wave-particle duality: Light and matter, when projected through two parallel slits, both have the potential to demonstrate the properties of either particles *or* waves, depending on the circumstances. In other words, matter might not be "matter" all the way down.

The science as it applies to the Microverse is simpler and looser: The smaller you get, the weirder things get.

> **FANTASTIC FACT!**
>
> *Microverses were originally assumed to be physically smaller universes existing within the atoms of our own macroverse. Now it's more commonly accepted that they are additional parallel universes, but that you access them by shrinking. Confusing? Yes. But if you can't get particular while literally discussing particles, what's the point of being a scientist?*

The Quantum Realm, loosely, is an umbrella term for multiverses, which are universes most easily accessed via shrinking, usually through the use of Pym Particles—subatomic particles created by founding Avenger, and the first Ant Man, Dr. Henry "Hank" Pym that allow for altering a person's (or object's) size and mass. Hence the original misconception that these were merely smaller worlds within our universe. Shrinking using Pym Particles triggers a rapid and extreme compression of matter that, in turn, generates a temporary artificial dimensional nexus transporting you to the Quantum Realm. You're not getting smaller *to* go to a tiny universe; you're getting smaller *and* going to a tiny universe. It's simple if you think about it—and way simpler if you don't.

## WHAT ARE PYM PARTICLES?

As with all things shrinking, the cause and solution to your problems lie in Pym Particles. Matter in the Marvel Universe is comprised not only of protons, neutrons, and electrons, but the subatomic particle known as kirbons, which are what actually give matter its size, mass, and density. Hank Pym discovered these particles and modified them for safe manipulation on and within the human body—eponymously renaming this proprietary version Pym Particles.

> **FANTASTIC FACT!**
>
> *This is the exact kind of thing Hank Pym would do.*

> **TONY'S TECH TIP!**
>
> *You named yourself Mister Fantastic.*

> **USE YOUR SPIDER-SENSE!**
>
> *Mom, Dad, please don't fight.*

Pym Particles work by disassembling and reassembling the matter of living organisms at nearly light speed, not unlike some methods of mechanical teleportation. However, instead of reassembling the organism at its original dimensions, a smaller version is constructed. Whether or not this constitutes the destruction of the original person and the creation of a copy, as it may with certain forms of teleportation, is a philosophical matter best not considered for very long by people who need to use Pym Particles for work.

## LET'S GET BIG

The Quantum Realm is a fun place to visit, but based on the relative sanity of the permanent residents, you wouldn't want to live there. Follow these steps to leave in a big hurry:

1. ***Prepare Your Pym Particles:*** Originally developed in the form of a serum, Pym Particles are now deployed as a gas, usually in an Ant-Man-style communication and breathing apparatus.

2. ***Get Some Elbow Room:*** On this level, you're not *actually* rapidly expanding as much as teleporting to another dimension, but it's still considered polite to warn others to take a few steps back, especially if they're holding drinks.

3. ***Activate Pym Particles:*** Growth to original size will be near instantaneous. You may feel a certain lightheadedness, which is ironic because your head is now billions of times heavier than it was one second ago. Such is physics.

WHEN LEAVING THE QUANTUM REALM, MAKE SURE YOU KNOW WHERE YOU'RE GOING: PICK A SPOT IN YOUR OWN PATCH OF THE MULTIVERSE WITH PLENTY OF ELBOW ROOM.

## SUB-ATOMICA: THE TINY FRONTIER

Traveling the Quantum Realm is a lot like visiting outer space but much, *much* weirder. Many miniature Marvel adventures are centered around Sub-Atomica, a microscopic star system that includes the following worlds:

- *MIRWOOD:* A tiny, vaguely medieval planet, once briefly ruled by Doctor Doom, as most things eventually are.
- *TOK:* Sworn enemy of Mirwood, populated by muscular lizard men in little shorts. You can't miss them.
- *TRAAN:* Facing an overpopulation crisis, Traan was vulnerable to takeover by its chief scientist, the emotion-manipulating tyrant known as . . .

## PSYCHO-MAN

One of the most persistent sworn enemies of the Fantastic Four (which is saying something), Psycho-Man is arguably the most famous denizen of the Quantum Realm. Using his Control Box—a device for manipulating the emotions of his enemies—Psycho-Man became obsessed with conquering Earth to solve his planet's overpopulation crisis. Although it remains unclear why conquering Earth was necessary at all, considering the entire population of his planet could easily fit on the head of a pin.

> **FANTASTIC FACT!**
>
> *Looking for logic in the actions of super villains is often an overly generous exercise.*

# SO WHO YOU GONNA CALL? THE RIGHT HEROES FOR THE CRISIS

> "THEY ALL PUT THEIR TIGHTS ON THE SAME WAY YOU DO: ONE LEG AT A TIME. YOU WOULDN'T HAVE BEEN CALLED UP IF THEY DIDN'T THINK YOU COULD CUT IT."
> – SPIDER-MAN, *THE INFINITY GAUNTLET*, VOL. 1, #3

Something you hear a lot in the Marvel Universe is "This is not their fight." Sure, that might sound like a convenient explanation for why Doctor Strange doesn't help out Spider-Man every time by teleporting the Green Goblin into the Dark Dimension with a wave of his hand.

### USE YOUR SPIDER-SENSE!

*Little help, Doc?*

Actually, it's a very logical strategic principle: "Stay in your lane." If Doctor Strange is occupied helping Spider-Man every time, he won't be free to stop the Mindless Ones, who end up becoming the problem of the Fantastic Four, which frees up Doctor Doom to attack the Avengers, which busies them so Loki can mess with

Moon Knight—and so on, until all Earth's heroes are spread thin, facing villains they may know nothing about. Including how best to defeat them.[1]

This is why Marvel heroes tend to have "beats"—areas of crime-fighting/world-saving expertise that they focus on without tripping over each other between team-ups. Here's how to match the right crisis to the right heroes:

### GLOBAL THREAT:
**S.H.I.E.L.D.** (threats may include terrorist groups, android duplicates, and advanced psychedelic imagery)

### GALACTIC THREAT:
**The Guardians of the Galaxy** (threats may include Annihilation Waves, Space Kings, or Symbiote Dragons)

### UNIVERSAL THREAT:
**The Avengers** (threats may include Infinity Gauntlets, sentient robot apocalypses, or wars between intergalactic empires)

### MULTIVERSAL THREAT:
**The Fantastic Four** (threats may include interdimensional incursions, invading Negative Zone hordes, or Doctor Doom becoming god-emperor of reality)

### OMNIVERSAL THREAT:
**The Defenders** (threats may include time-traveling wizards unraveling history, sentient universes, or Galactus's flirty mom[2])

---

[1] Further reading: Marvel's *Acts of Vengeance* event.
[2] Further reading: *Defenders*, Vol. 6.

***MUTANT THREAT:***
**The X-Men, X-Force, Excalibur, X-Factor, Generation X, The Exiles, X-Corp, Weapon X, The X-Men of 2099, Academy X, The X-Terminators, X-Statix** (threats include militant mutants, even more militant mutant-haters, and Sentinels; if people still used phonebooks, you could pretty much just turn to X and pick a team to help you)

***WEST COAST THREAT:***
**The West Coast Avengers** (threats may include tech billionaires, Hollywood execs, or green smoothies that fail to advertise they are merely vegetarian and not vegan)

***CANADIAN THREAT:***
**Alpha Flight** (threats may include snow, butter tarts, or impoliteness; team *will* include Wolverine and/or Deadpool)

***CHILDHOOD-LEVEL THREATS:***
**The Power Pack** (threats may include bullies, aliens, or alien bullies)

***ADOLESCENT-LEVEL THREATS:***
**The Runaways** (threats may include evil parents, secretly evil teens, secretly *not* evil teens, and time travel)

***YOUNG ADULT–LEVEL THREATS:***
**The Champions** (threats may include . . . basically the same stuff adult super heroes have to deal with, but without anyone taking you seriously)

# SO YOU'RE DEALING WITH MAGIC

> "Magic is taking a thought and making it real. Taking a lie and making it the truth. Telling a story to the universe so utterly, cosmically perfect that for a single, shining moment . . . the world believes a man can fly."
> – LOKI, *LOKI: AGENT OF ASGARD*, VOL. 1, #1

Magic is real. And we don't mean in the laughter of a child or the path of the rainbow as it arcs across the sky, although the metaphorically magical feelings elicited by those things are potent conceptual ingredients in *actual* magic (stay with us).

We mean that in the Marvel Universe, magic and magicians—and witches, sorcerers, and gods—are all real. As are gods and mutants who also practice magic, in addition to their latent superhuman abilities. So if you've recently acquired magical powers, or if you're dealing with an enemy who has, step right up. We're looking for a volunteer. Nothing up our sleeves—except *everything you can imagine*.

## WHAT IS MAGIC?

Across universes, the term *magic* essentially refers to an umbrella term for the spiritual practice of applying one's actions and intent toward the indirect manipulation of reality. In more mundane universes, that might mean performing a ritual to focus your intention and project it onto the universe, or attempting to manifest a desired outcome using positive thought. In the Marvel Universe, that means tracing complicated patterns in the air with your fingers and reciting dramatic incantations to open portals or project energy bolts—usually toward someone else doing the same thing at you.

*Magic* (or *Magik*, if you're referring to the super hero name used by Illyana Rasputin of the New Mutants) is where art, science, and religiosity intersect to attempt to control forces that many believe we can perceive and experience—like luck, déjà vu, and coincidence—but that cannot be controlled by known scientific means.

---

### TONY'S TECH TIP!

*Magic. I don't buy it (and I can afford to buy a lot).*
*Magic is just science we don't understand yet.*

---

## MAGIC VS. SUPER-POWERS

At a glance, magic seems indistinguishable from garden-variety super-powers. After all, what's casting a fireball spell other than releasing a concentrated burst of cosmic ray–activated pyrokinesis? There are two major differences:

### *SOURCE*
Magic is an extant extra-dimensional force (or forces) that is always present and can theoretically be tapped into by anyone. While many super-powers strongly *resemble* magic—like Storm's control over the weather—these rely on, and are typically constrained by, the physics of our universe. Super-powers are ultimately finite power sets, scientifically explicable, and linked to the hero's particular genetic alteration (e.g., Spider-Man was bitten by a spider and now has spider-powers).

Magic is *without* limit or definition, and with the right tools and know-how, a powerful magic user could also control the weather *and* turn you into a spider, in addition to infinitely more supernatural acts.

### *COST*
With magic, there's always a price. Whereas mutants, like Storm, draw upon their internal stamina and the limits of their (albeit superhuman) bodies, magic users who have no innate abilities must come by their power the old-fashioned way: spoken incantations, precise hand gestures, potions and chemical reactions, and magical artifacts (see "Magical Artifacts" on page 102).

In addition to the baseline cost of learning these skills and collecting these resources, magic itself is not free. The parallel dimensions that contain it are analogous to oil wells. Sometimes you're tapping into one already claimed by someone powerful. Other times, you mess with forces you can't control and start a fire that consumes you.

There is also a bit of overlap in the Venn diagram of super-powers vs. magic powers. Many magic users are *adepts*—naturally gifted magic users who often discover their talents accidentally, not unlike a mutant coming into their powers. To these gifted mortals, magic comes more easily, and they often become powerful Masters of the Mystic Arts. Some prominent adepts include Billy Kaplan, a.k.a. Wiccan, a reincarnated son of the Scarlet Witch, and the Asgardian God of Various Mostly Bad Things: Loki (see "Fine, Let's Talk About Loki" on page 105).

## THE SORCERER SUPREME

In the Marvel Universe, Sorcerer or Sorceress Supreme is an honorific and profound duty bestowed by the universe's own magical forces upon whichever magic user currently holds the most magical skill or naturally commands the most magical power in that universe. The most famous of these is Doctor Strange, but other sorcerers to hold the title include his companion Clea, Doctor Doom, the supernatural hero Brother Voodoo, and—again—Loki.

Other universes, like the Dark Dimension and the Hell-like dimension of Limbo, or other natural forces—such as the concept of Death—also have their own Sorcerer and Sorceress Supremes. However, these, too, frequently turn out to be Clea and Doctor Strange.

## MAGICAL ARTIFACTS

The Marvel Universe, for having so many scientists in it, is also swarming with magical artifacts. If you wish to become a Marvel magic user—or just want to step up your current magic game—you can do so by acquiring a legendary relic like the ones on this list:

***THE DARKHOLD:*** An ancient grimoire (magical spellbook) written in flesh (then again in stone, and finally in parchment) by the evil Elder God Chthon. Handed down through the eons, the forbidden magics contained by the Darkhold have shaped history, usually for the worse. Copies have been wielded by such legendary magic users as the Scarlet Witch, Doctor Doom, and Agatha Harkness. A copy in possession of the Vatican was once nearly acquired by Dracula. Yes, that Dracula. From *Dracula*.

***THE EYE OF AGAMOTTO:*** Originally used by, and named for, Earth's first Sorcerer Supreme, Agamotto. The Eye of Agamotto is a mystical amulet, typically worn by Doctor Strange. The Eye lets its wearer track ethereal beings, project beams that weaken enemies, and see through illusions. This last part is especially useful, since illusions are a go-to move by magic-using villains, particularly the Asgardian God of Evil / Mischief / Lies / Stories / Outcasts / Stories Again—known as Loki.

***THE CRIMSON GEM OF CYTTORAK:*** Also named for an ancient magical entity (are you magically sensing a pattern?). This powerful demon (or god, depending on who's asking) is an embodiment of rage and destruction who, in a wager with other

**MAGICAL ARTIFACTS COME WITH A COST:** BEFORE YOU TRY TO USE THEM, MAKE SURE THE RISKS ARE WORTH THE POWER-UP!

**THE DARKHOLD:** BEWARE ITS CORRUPTING MAGIC.

**THE EYE OF AGAMOTTO:** MAY GROW A THIRD EYE ON YOUR FOREHEAD.

**THE CRIMSON GEM OF CYTTORAK:** GRANTS THE UNSTOPPABLE POWER OF PURE RAGE.

**THE EBONY BLADE:** BEARS THE CURSE OF BLOODLUST.

**THE CASKET OF ANCIENT WINTERS:** UNLEASHES ENDLESS WINTER.

ancient demons/gods, created the Gem of Cyttorak. Touching it transformed its discoverer (and many who came after) into the superstrong, unstoppable X-Men villain (or ally, depending on who's asking) known as Juggernaut.

> ### FANTASTIC FACT!
>
> *Doctor Strange and other sorcerers can also summon the Crimson Bands of Cyttorak, which are sort of like unbreakable magic ribbons to entangle foes or keep people out of Wong's kitchen—a.k.a. any kitchen where Wong is cooking. Wong is . . . serious about that.[1]*

**THE EBONY BLADE:** Forged from a meteorite, this sword has been enchanted to protect its user from death, cut through anything, and repel magical attacks, but at the cost of slowly driving those who wield it insane with bloodlust. Passed down through the generations, it is typically wielded by a lineage of heroes calling themselves the Black Knight—the first Black Knight having helped forge the sword with Merlin. Yes, that Merlin. It's always the one you're thinking of.

**THE CASKET OF ANCIENT WINTERS:** We mentioned weather control. The Casket of Ancient Winters is one of the most powerful weapons in Odin's Asgardian armory. This small chest, when opened, releases a giant, never-ending snowstorm with

---

[1] Further reading: *The New Avengers*, Vol. 2, #7.

the deadly force of hundreds of winters. Okay, it's not so much controlling the weather as unleashing weather *no one* can control. For obvious reasons, it's a favorite weapon of the Asgardians' ancient foes, the Frost Giants, including their most famous family member—do I even need to say it?—Loki.

## FINE, LET'S TALK ABOUT LOKI
Since he keeps coming up. As he does.

There are a few immutable laws in the Marvel Universe that are not *technically* magic but feel like cosmic rules: The Hulk will smash. Namor will declare war on the surface world. And Loki will Loki.

A Frost Giant of the frozen realm of Jotunheim, Loki was cast out as an infant for his tiny (read: human-sized) stature. Found abandoned, Loki was then adopted by the sworn enemy of the Frost Giants, Odin—King of Asgard, All-Father of the Norse Gods, and father to Loki's now-brother, Thor. Whereas Thor excelled in all things Asgardian (fighting, being large), Loki was slight and sensitive and quickly became bitter about living in the shadow of Asgard's golden (haired) boy.

Loki, growing up as no one thing, taught himself to be many things—and eventually, many Lokis. Finding himself adept at magic, he studied day and night to learn the mystical skills and spells that would make him the better of his arrogant brother. If not in a fight, then in a scheme.

## LOKI'S POWERS

As a Frost Giant anointed with godhood by Odin, Loki possesses the baseline powers of an Asgardian god, including the following:

- **ENHANCED STRENGTH AND DURABILITY** (compared with humans, but not Thors)
- **EFFECTIVE AGELESSNESS AND IMMORTALITY**
- **ENERGY MANIPULATION** (details vary, but one example: summoning the Bifrost)

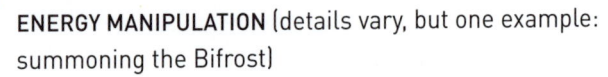

Loki supplements these powers with rigorously studied magical spells and abilities including, but not limited to, the following:

- **SHAPE-SHIFTING**
- **ILLUSION CASTING** (including over self, which is *like* shape-shifting, but different)
- **ASTRAL PROJECTION**
- **TELEPORTATION** (often via portals)
- **HYPNOSIS**

This last one is particularly insulting given how much effort Loki puts into manipulating others into doing his bidding *without* the brute force of hypnosis. If lying is a game to Loki, he enjoys excelling at it too much to use a cheat code.

## HOW TO DEFEAT LOKI

Fortunately, this is relatively straightforward. The only downside is that a colossal amount of damage is usually done first. The steps to defeating Loki are as follows:

1. WAIT FOR HIM TO FAIL.
2. HIT HIM.

---

### USE YOUR SPIDER-SENSE!

*Don't trust Loki. You're going to. Repeatedly. In spite of yourself. You'll see yourself doing it and think to yourself, "This is a bad idea." It's inevitable. But I still need to say this out loud: Don't.*

# SO YOU'RE FACING A DOOMBOT

> "HEY!!? IT'S NOTHIN' BUT A ROBOT!"
> – THE THING, *FANTASTIC FOUR*, VOL. 1, #5

Victor von Doom: despotic ruler of Latveria, super-genius scientist, Master of the Mystic Arts, occasional wielder of the Power Cosmic, and sometime Sorcerer Supreme. Sworn enemy of Reed Richards and the Fantastic Four, Doctor Doom is the Marvel Universe's preeminent super villain and the most terrifying foe you are likely to meet.

So it's good news that you're not likely to actually meet him.

Dressing head to toe in high-tech armor comes with a number of benefits: obvious defensive capabilities, endless hidden weaponry, a vanity-protecting face mask, and—crucially—being indistinguishable from a robot. To maintain his busy lifestyle of oppressing an entire nation, conquering an entire planet, and insulating himself from countless enemies, Doctor Doom liberally deploys Doombots—high-tech robot doppelgängers of his own invention—to serve as decoys, henchmen, and disposable soldiers. If you encounter "Doctor Doom," you most likely didn't—but that doesn't mean the danger isn't real. Here's how to send one of Victor's platinum Pinocchios back to Latveria in pieces.

## DETECTING A DOOMBOT

It's a Doombot.

BUT—

It's always a Doombot.

## DEFEATING A DOOMBOT

Doombots are robots built by Doctor Doom, which is a double-edged sword.* Even a design by Victor von Doom reveals flaws once it's mass-produced at the level he requires. And programming an AI with your own megalomaniacal ego can have its drawbacks. Memorize these Doombot-dismantling techniques to live long enough to get on the real Doom's bad side.

> **TONY'S TECH TIP!**
>
> *As a sometime blacksmith, I've never understood this expression. Double-edged swords are just swords with symmetrical blades—like common broadswords and short swords—as opposed to single-edged swords, like cutlasses and katanas. I find that as long as it's pointed at the other guy, there's actually not much of a downside. It's double-pointed swords you need to look out for.

SIGNS TO TELL THE DIFFERENCE BETWEEN DOCTOR DOOM AND DOOMBOT: REALISTICALLY, THESE APPLY TO BOTH, SO PREPARE FOR A FIGHT EITHER WAY.

***SHORT-CIRCUIT IT:*** Doombots may be heavily armored, but that defends only against physical attacks. Technology-disrupting abilities—like the intangible "phasing" of the X-Men's Kitty Pryde—can scramble a Doombot's circuitry, reducing it to a fashionably caped junk heap. Similarly, a Doombot being operated remotely by Doom himself is receiving signals. Hijack that frequency with a stronger signal at a closer proximity and you just got yourself a free Doombot.

***PSYCH IT OUT:*** Doctor Doom programs Doombots to believe they are the real Victor von Doom before he unleashes them into the world to pursue his goals. Only in the presence of other Doombots or Doom himself does the Doom personality take a back seat—leaving the Doombot with no memory that it ever believed itself to be real. But as with all androids, an existential paradox is right around the corner. The Doom personality template comes complete with his hypercompetitive ego, and questioning the robot's status as "real" could manipulate it into glitching out and even challenging its master for supremacy. One warning: Whether triggered by a classic android freak-out or Doom's own fail-safes, this method typically ends in self-destruction.**

---

### TONY'S TECH TIP!

*\*\*Another misleading term. The "self" being destructed here is just as likely to be you.*

***PUNCH IT:*** This is the favorite method of Doctor Doom's frequent foe Benjamin J. Grimm, the Fantastic Four's ever-lovin' blue-eyed Thing. Like most sophisticated electronics, Doombots still go down when you smash them with a rock.

## FACING MULTIPLE DOOMBOTS

As aforementioned, Doombots are just as likely to appear in swarms. If this happens, you have a much narrower list of options, and you'd be wise to act quickly.

***EGO CONTEST:*** As with a single Doombot, you may be able to convince one or more that they are the real Doctor Doom, coaxing them into overriding their own programming. This will ignite a chain-reaction debate over which Doombot is the true supreme ruler of Latveria and beyond—but this is where you make a graceful exit before that "debate" escalates into concussive palm blasts.

***AN EMP:*** A tried-and-true method of mass robot disposal, an EMP—or electromagnetic pulse—is a technology-wiping burst of electromagnetic radiation. Like gamma radiation, EMPs can be generated naturally by solar flares and lightning strikes or, less naturally, by high-atmosphere nuclear weapons that can permanently destroy the power grid below while (somewhat) minimizing the death and destruction caused by the explosion and subsequent radiation. For this reason, the Marvel Universe's EMPs tend to be radiation-free affairs, activated by various high-tech gizmos. Always pack gizmos.

**BE WOLVERINE:** This strategy works in most situations, but it works especially well in melee combat against multiple nonliving opponents who can ethically be shredded by adamantium claws. This might include Doombots, Ultrons, Sentinels, zombies, and Hand clan ninjas (who are essentially zombies). Vampires and plant-based organisms are a gray area.

> **FANTASTIC FACT!**
>
> *My working theory is that Victor's armor is powered by his hatred for me. This isn't a joke. I know how this could be accomplished (cranial psionic energy collector panels). Talk about renewable energy.*

# PART THREE

# *DAY-TO-DAY*

# SO YOUR CAT IS A FLERKEN

> *"I NEED YOU TO NOT BE UNDERFOOT RIGHT NOW."*
> – CAPTAIN MARVEL, *CAPTAIN MARVEL*, VOL. 8, #7

They're the weirdest, most unpredictable, and most disgusting species in the Marvel Universe—cats.

But believe it or not, there are some species out there that are almost as strange and disgusting as house cats. Take, for example, their outer-space lookalikes: the spring-loaded, tentacle-mouthed aliens known as Flerkens.

If you've recently picked up a stray from outer space, here's what you need to know about the care and feeding of your new exotic (*very* exotic) pet.

### USE YOUR SPIDER-SENSE!

*Flerkens and cats are so similar that anyone with cat allergies should pack their antihistamines before leaving Earth. In space, no one can hear you sneeze.*

## WHAT IS A FLERKEN?

Indistinguishable from Earth house cats until they exhibit alien behavior, Flerkens are most recognizable once they've unleashed their most distinguishing alien feature—a blossoming mass of slimy prehensile tentacles they keep ultra-compressed in their nested mouths.

Flerkens come in all the same shapes, sizes, and colors of Earth cats but contain multitudes. This is not a metaphor—Flerken bodies hold pocket dimensions (see "So You're Lost in the Multiverse"), allowing them to temporarily consume and store virtually anything, including living beings, safely and intact, albeit covered with pinkish slime. This "bigger on the inside" quirk of their biological metaphysics may also explain why the tentacles they contain appear larger than the mass of the cat that protruded them. Flerkens use their tentacles for offensive and defensive capabilities, mobility, and to wrangle the objects or organisms they swallow into their internal subspace storage. Assuming they don't just *actually* eat them.

In addition to transporting living beings inside their bodies, Flerkens can utilize their own interior pocket dimensions for *self*-teleportation, with or without a passenger. However, this still fails to distinguish them significantly from regular cats, who also have the ability to randomly appear in a room without you knowing how they got there.

> **FANTASTIC FACT!**
>
> *In at least one Multiverse, all Flerken bodies lead to the same pocket dimension, meaning that long-distance travel is theoretically possible by allowing yourself to be swallowed by one Flerken and regurgitated by another. All versions of Flerken teleportation result in being covered with "goop"; therefore, none are advisable for a daily commute.*

## HUMAN INTELLIGENCE

Though not capable of speech, Flerkens appear to have human intelligence and can fully understand humans. In this way they differ from Earth cats, who erroneously believe they have higher-than-human intelligence and pretend *not* to be able to understand us.

## CARE AND FEEDING

Many Flerkens go unidentified due to the convenient fact that they can happily survive on cat food. In most ways, a Flerken that is not challenged or threatened in any way will have all the same needs as an ordinary cat. That is, until . . .

## REPRODUCTION

Flerkens reproduce asexually by laying, in at least one known example, upward of a hundred eggs. Should this occur, rather than disturb the Flerken parent by approaching its nest, you have two options:

🥚 ALLOW THE EGGS TO HATCH AND TEND TO THE NEWBORN FLERKENS, FINDING INDIVIDUAL LOVING HOMES FOR THEM OR ALLOWING THEM TO MATURE TO THE POINT OF INDEPENDENTLY TELEPORTING AWAY.

🥚 TAKE THE EGGS TO A PET SHELTER THAT CAN ACCOMMODATE INTERGALACTIC CREATURES.

**PREPARE FOR FLERKEN CARE:**
BE READY FOR UNUSUAL HAIRBALLS FROM A POCKET DIMENSION AND TO REPLACE A LOT OF FOOD BOWLS.

# SO YOU THINK YOU'VE FOUND A SKRULL

> "WE ARE PREPARED TO ACCEPT YOUR SURRENDER."
>
> – SKRULL IMPERSONATING EDWIN JARVIS, *SECRET INVASION*, VOL. 1, #4

Sometimes Marvel heroes go to space. Sometimes space comes to them. One of the earliest and most enduring threats to emerge at the beginning of the Marvel age is the race of shape-shifting alien invaders known as the Skrulls. They can look like anyone. Many of them can replicate super-powers. And they have one consistent goal: invasion. If you suspect that someone in your life may be a secret Skrull, here's how to find out—and what to do about it.

## WHAT ARE SKRULLS?

Originating eons ago on the planet Skrullos in the Andromeda galaxy, Skrulls are green-skinned aliens with the power to shape-shift and impersonate anyone (or anything). In their true form, Skrulls typically have long, pointy ears and distinct vertical ridges on their chins. Born warriors and conquerors, the Skrulls aggressively colonized other worlds, building the oldest empire in the known universe.

> **FANTASTIC FACT!**
>
> *Some of the earliest Skrulls to be identified on Earth were diminutive in stature, possibly giving rise to the stereotype of aliens as "little green men."*

Obsessive tinkerers in their own biology, Skrulls eventually learned how to use genetic engineering and technological enhancement to replicate and surpass the abilities of superhumans. These enhanced Skrulls are known as . . .

## SUPER-SKRULLS

Elite soldiers and spies of the Skrull empire, Super-Skrulls have been augmented or engineered to replicate the super-powers of beings they have encountered. After the Fantastic Four defeated a Skrull reconnaissance team ahead of a potential invasion, the empire pursued revenge with the first known Super-Skrull, Kl'rt, who possessed both the Skrull ability to shape-shift and the combined powers of the Fantastic Four. Years later, armies of sleeper-agent Super-Skrulls posing as humans were activated in a full-scale Secret Invasion of Earth.

On the plus side, afterward, many kidnapped heroes who had been replaced by Skrulls were suddenly returned to Earth with clean slates. So if you ever embarrassed yourself at a party or acted super weird during a breakup—no you didn't. A Skrull *pretending* to be you did. And it's very rude to accuse you of lying after what you've been through.

## IDENTIFYING A SKRULL

Before the upgrades of the Secret Invasion Super-Skrulls, there were any number of conventional ways to sniff out a Skrull impostor—in one case, actually by sniffing:

***SUPER-SENSES:*** A powerful sense of smell, like Daredevil's or Wolverine's, could identify the difference between a Skrull and a human—assuming the smeller knew what a Skrull smelled like to begin with.

***TELEPATHY:*** Invasive mind reading, if available, was likely the easiest way to identify a Skrull. This meant invading the privacy of the target without asking permission, but telepaths in the Marvel Universe rarely had a problem with this.

***MEDICAL SCANNING:*** If you were able to incapacitate the suspect long enough to get them to hold still, comprehensive medical scanning might have revealed internal biological differences. And if you were wrong but caught early cancer, they would probably forgive you.

During the events of the Secret Invasion, Mister Fantastic created a device capable of revealing the newly upgraded, undetectable Skrulls. However, the Skrulls responded by upgrading yet again, leaving humanity back at square one.

When all else fails, Skrulls revert to their original form after death. But if you find a Skrull who has passed on, the whole question is likely moot.

**PICKING SKRULLS OUT OF A CROWD CAN BE CHALLENGING:** SKRULLS CAN SECRETLY TAKE THE FORM OF ANYONE THEY WANT, EVEN YOUR FAVORITE HEROES!

# SO YOUR JOB MAY BE A FRONT FOR HYDRA

> "MY GOD...I'VE BEEN WORKING FOR YOU THE ENTIRE TIME."
> – BARON VON STRUCKER, SECRET WARRIORS, VOL. 1, #26

Mondays, am I right? It's like you knock one out and four more workdays just pop up to replace it.

The above bit of extremely funny office humor is, of course, a play on the official slogan of the Marvel Universe's premiere evil, secret terrorist organization, Hydra:

*"Hail Hydra! Immortal Hydra!*
*We shall never be destroyed!*
*Cut off a limb, and two more shall take its place!"*

Probably looks great on the free coffee mugs. What Hydra is revealing about themselves with this battle cry is their primary strategy for global domination: recruitment.

Hydra aggressively builds its ranks to make good on the threat of replacing any fallen soldier with two more (think of them as a slightly more evil MLM). Any Marvel hero who has battled Hydra can attest to this. The rank-and-file Hydra agents are largely just regular folks—but there are always, *always* more of them.

But beyond strength in numbers, Hydra's other modus operandi, not unlike the Skrulls (see "So You've Found a Skrull"), is infiltration. Creeping its way into an organization—a government, a Stark tech subsidiary, an ordinary workplace like yours—and taking it over from within. Replacing, recruiting, or brainwashing the personnel one by one until only Hydra zealots remain.

Of course, the funny thing about going "one by one" is that someone has to be the last to know. If you suspect you're the only real employee left at a Hydra cell, this chapter will help you find out for certain.

## WHAT IS HYDRA?

In its earliest incarnation, Hydra was one half of an ancient global organization created to protect the world from outside and supernatural threats: the Brotherhood of the Spear and the Brotherhood of the Shield. Today, S.H.I.E.L.D. remains a global spy agency primarily affiliated with the democratic world and ostensibly fighting on the side of the good guys, while the Spear morphed into Hydra, a cultlike paramilitary organization now fully bent on domination through infiltration and force.

Probably at your job.

**OFF-TOPIC EMAILS FROM COWORKERS**

"OFF TOPIC"
FROM: MGMT
TO: ALL

**MYSTERIOUS DOORS WITH ALARMS**

**ANTI-S.H.I.E.L.D. PROPAGANDA**

**MANDATORY GREEN UNIFORMS**

SIGNS YOU MIGHT BE WORKING FOR A HYDRA CELL:
YOU CAN'T ALWAYS RELY ON HEARING "HAIL HYDRA" AT THE WATERCOOLER, SO KEEP AN EYE OUT FOR SUBTLER CLUES.

## SIGNS YOU MIGHT BE WORKING FOR A HYDRA CELL

Here's a list of telltale clues that you are unknowingly working for a secret front of a global terrorist organization. Check off as many as apply to your workplace:

- FORCED TO PICK UP OTHER PEOPLE'S SLACK, LIKE THEY MIGHT BE DISTRACTED.
- BOSSES WHO SEEM SUSPICIOUSLY UNQUALIFIED FOR THE JOBS THEY HAVE.
- LONG, EXHAUSTING MEETINGS WHERE NOTHING IS ACCOMPLISHED EXCEPT THE BREAKING OF YOUR SPIRIT.
- COWORKERS ENGAGING IN BORING SMALL TALK (as though hiding details about their lives).
- NONE OF THE TECHNOLOGY WORKS CORRECTLY.
- YOU'RE THE ONLY PERSON WHO MAKES COFFEE.
- PHYSICAL ACTIVITY IS ENCOURAGED (calisthenics, company picnics, and field days).
- ANTI-S.H.I.E.L.D. POSTER IN THE BREAKROOM.
- MANDATORY UNIFORM OF IDENTICAL GREEN JUMPSUITS.
- COWORKERS, IN UNISON, CONSTANTLY SHOUT, "HAIL HYDRA! WE WORK FOR HYDRA!"

If you checked off more than three of these boxes, quit your job immediately without telling anyone and report to the nearest S.H.I.E.L.D. offices.

# SO YOU NEED TO LIFT THOR'S HAMMER

> "THERE'S PLENTY ONE MAN CAN DO—
> IF HE IS THE RIGHT MAN."
> – CAPTAIN AMERICA, *THOR*, VOL. 1, #390

There's an old saying: When the only tool you have is a hammer, every problem looks like a nail. Some hammers are so powerful that they actually *can* solve every problem. That is, if you can pick them up.

It happens all the time in the Marvel Universe. Against all odds, the mightiest of the Avengers,* Thor Odinson—Prince of Asgard, the God of Thunder—has been felled by some cosmic-level threat. Thor's short-handled war hammer, Mjolnir, for all purposes a part of his own body, now lies discarded at his side, half buried in the concrete, heavier than physics should allow. Because it's not *physical* weight that's keeping it down but the weight of responsibility on whoever should hold it.

## WHOSOEVER HOLDS THIS HAMMER, IF HE BE WORTHY, SHALL POSSESS THE POWER OF THOR.

If Thor is down, the rest of the Avengers probably are too, having given it their all. But the villain is on the ropes! One decisive blow with the Marvel Universe's most powerful handheld weapon might be enough to flatten the bad guy and save the universe. And you *happen* to be walking by. The fate of the world is potentially in your hands. The question is . . . are you worthy? If you're not sure, reading this chapter is the first step.

> **FANTASTIC FACT!**
>
> \* Mightiest, *not* strongest. *The difference seems arbitrary, but there's one Avenger who gets very angry if you don't call him "the strongest." Angry enough to repeatedly prove it to several blocks of Manhattan.*

## WHAT IS MJOLNIR?

As it so often does, it all started with a prank by Loki. Long story short, some youthful godly indiscretions resulted in the commission of multiple weapons and treasures by the Ten Realms' greatest blacksmiths, Eitri and the Dwarves of Nidavellir. Among these was Mjolnir. It was intended to be a long-handled, two-handed war hammer, but Eitri was interrupted and could only make a short-handled hammer, better suited to be held in one hand—or thrown. This design quirk hasn't presented any practical problems so far.

> **FANTASTIC FACT!**
>
> *The forging of Mjolnir and the breaking of its mold cast off asteroid-like fireballs across the universe, some of which are rumored to have caused the extinction of the dinosaurs. Not a very "worthy" thing to do, in the opinion of this scientist.*

Mjolnir is made of uru, a rare and indestructible enchanted metal, rumored to be the same material that comprised the universe's first moon (see "Moon Knight" on page 136). Uru comes in two known consistencies: a rough, iron-gray form (as in Mjolnir) or a polished gold form, as in hammers forged later and some crowns worn by Loki. It's very logical, in hindsight, that Loki would look at Thor's prized possession and think, "I want one too, but make mine shinier."

## BECOMING WORTHY

Arrogant in his youth, Thor endured multiple trials imposed by his less-than-gentle parent, Odin, who repeatedly forced him to humble himself, rededicate his life to service, and once again earn the purity of heart required to unlock his full powers as the God of Thunder and wield his greatest weapon.

Everyone wants to think they're worthy, but it actually takes a great deal of effort. Before you dislocate your shoulder by yanking on an unliftable hammer, take a mental tally of the following "worthy" actions. Do you . . .

- 🔨 CUT UP THE PLASTIC RINGS FROM SODA CANS SO THAT TURTLES DON'T GET STUCK IN THEM?
- 🔨 TEXT BEFORE CALLING?
- 🔨 MAKE SURE TO FACTOR IN TAX AND TIP BEFORE YOU PAY YOUR SHARE OF THE CHECK?
- 🔨 REMEMBER WHEN IT'S YOUR TURN TO BRING DONUTS ON FRIDAYS?
- 🔨 NOT CUT THE ENTIRE LINE AT THE UPS STORE BECAUSE YOU'RE "JUST DROPPING OFF A PACKAGE"—Everyone there is dropping off a package.
- 🔨 DONATE BLOOD, EVEN IF IT RISKS THE CREATION OF A SENSATIONAL SHE-HULK?
- 🔨 AT LEAST *THINK* ABOUT DOING MEATLESS MONDAYS?
- 🔨 RETURN YOUR BORROWED BOOKS ON TIME TO THE HALLS OF ALL-KNOWING—THE LIBRARY OF OMNIPOTENCE CITY?
- 🔨 ADOPT FROM SHELTERS RATHER THAN PURCHASE FROM DOG (OR FLERKEN) BREEDERS?
- 🔨 SWITCH TO ECO-FRIENDLY LIGHTBULBS, EVEN THOUGH THEY'RE MORE EXPENSIVE AND CHANGING THEM ALL IS A HASSLE?
- 🔨 RECYCLE YOUR CUT-UP PLASTIC RINGS?

If you checked every box above, it's hammer time.

## "LIFT WITH YOUR LEGS"

Just because you're worthy enough to lift Mjolnir doesn't mean it's going to be easy. Like any heavy object, use the following steps to lift Mjolnir safely so that the only injury is to the face of the person you swing it at:

1. ***Create a Stable Base:*** Sometimes called the "karate stance," your feet should be planted firmly on the ground, shoulder-width apart, with one foot slightly in front of the other.

2. ***Squat Maintaining Posture:*** Back straight, chin up, eyes ahead. Presumably on whatever Frost Giant or Kree Sentry is stomping toward you.

   Keeping that posture, bend at the knees to lower yourself via your hips and glutes toward the ground.

3. ***Slowly Lift:*** Pressing upward with your feet, reverse the squat, slowly raising yourself via your knees and hips without curving or twisting your back.

4. ***Say Something Cool:*** With Mjolnir now firmly in your grasp, metaphorically lift the spirits of anyone watching by saying something incredibly hardcore like, "Ultron, we would have words with thee."

## WHO ELSE HAS LIFTED THOR'S HAMMER?

Don't be intimidated or discouraged when it comes to lifting Mjolnir. For an enchanted hammer that can only be lifted by Thor, it's been lifted by a *lot* of people who are not Thor (or who lift it and then *become* Thors). The list of those worthy enough to borrow Mjolnir includes, but is not limited to, the following:

**BETA RAY BILL:** A noble alien hero who took on the mantle of Thor.

**CAPTAIN AMERICA:** To the surprise of no one.

**JANE FOSTER:** A longtime Thor companion who also took on the mantle of Thor.

**BLACK PANTHER:** Specifically, the *first* Black Panther, who fought alongside prehistoric Avengers during the archaeologically improbable era of one million BC.

**SQUIRREL GIRL:** Like we said—unbeatable. Not just in the sense of "never loses a fight," but also because she's generally the best.

**SAFELY WIELDING MJOLNIR:**
EVEN FOR THE WORTHY,
IT'S IMPORTANT TO LIFT WITH
YOUR LEGS.

CREATE A STABLE BASE

SQUAT MAINTAINING POSTURE

HAIL ASGARD!

SLOWLY LIFT

SAY SOMETHING COOL

## LOOPHOLES AND CHEATS

You don't necessarily need to be worthy to use Thor's hammer. A number of unsavory characters have found ways to lift or otherwise manipulate it without being squeaky clean:

**LOKI:** Having been enchanted by a "moral inversion," a temporarily heroic Loki was able to wield Mjolnir to fight a temporarily evil Thor.

**MOON KNIGHT:** Using his mystical connection to the moon—and, as it turns out, all moons—Moon Knight was able to command Mjolnir, as it was technically made of moon rock, stopping it midair and redirecting it toward Thor himself.

**RED HULK:** As Red Hulk, General "Thunderbolt" Ross manipulated gravity in order to "lift" Thor's hammer. This, and all of the above, are considered jerk moves, made by jerks.

> **FANTASTIC FACT!**
>
> *In one possible future (or alternate reality), an actually **heroic** Loki was seen wielding Mjolnir, defending human refugees on Mars from an Ultron-possessed Thor.*

# SO YOU'VE GOT LEGAL TROUBLE

> "DOES THE PHRASE 'REASONABLE DOUBT' MEAN ANYTHING TO YOU?"
> – MATT MURDOCK, *DAREDEVIL*, VOL. 2, #23

Being a super hero isn't strictly legal. For all your good intentions and lifesaving contributions to society, you are still technically a masked vigilante taking the law into your own hands. In your defense, the NYPD might be ill-equipped to take down a thirty-foot villain made of variable-density living sand.

On the other hand, if you knock him out by throwing a city bus at him, you may require a defense—of the legal variety. That's where super hero lawyers come in. Consult this chapter for the hows—and the whos—of hiring a super-powered lawyer in the Marvel Universe.

## BEFORE YOU HIRE AN ATTORNEY

There's a legal term—*exposure*. Basically, it refers to how vulnerable your actions or circumstances have made you to legal or civil consequences. A good lawyer can mitigate your exposure. A bad lawyer can make it much, much worse. Ask the following questions when interviewing a prospective attorney, super or otherwise:

⚖️ **Do They Have Malpractice or Liability Insurance?**
If they don't want to answer—they do not.

⚖️ **How Quickly Are They Able to Return Your Calls?**
Since you need a lawyer, let's assume they *should* be calls and not emails.

⚖️ **Do They Offer Alternative Fee Structures?**
Options might include pro bono work, a sliding scale based on client income, or narrowing the scope of their services (e.g., bare bones vs. hands-on).

And ideally, the reason you need a lawyer does not include the phrases "hands-on" or "bare bones."

## MARVELOUS ATTORNEYS

In the Marvel Universe, these are your two most obvious choices for legal representation in the field of super hero law:

**Matt Murdock,** who practices law by day and patrols the rooftops of Hell's Kitchen by night as the super-senses-enhanced masked vigilante known as **Daredevil**.

**She-Hulk,** a.k.a. **Jennifer Walters**, who also practices law by day and who—day or night—uses her gamma-enhanced strength to protect the innocent in her non-secret identity of . . . She-Hulk.

WHICH ATTORNEYS SHOULD YOU HIRE?
WE'LL LET THEIR ADS SPEAK FOR THEMSELVES!

## SUPER P.I.s

Sometimes you can avoid legal trouble altogether by handling your problem quietly. Unfortunately, the Marvel Universe's private detectives aren't great at subtlety. While virtually all super heroes do some amount of private investigation, at least two are licensed: Jessica Jones and (using the term *super hero* very loosely) Howard the Duck.

**ALIAS INVESTIGATIONS**

**Jessica Jones**

Infidelity. Missing Persons. Fraud

485 W 46th St
New York, NY 10036

\* Will not respond to queries about Jewel

**Interns Wanted**

*The Daily Bugle* is looking

**CHOOSE YOUR P.I. WISELY:**
YOUR EXPERIENCE WITH ONE INVESTIGATOR MAY BE MORE DOWN TO EARTH, WHILE THE OTHER IS, WELL . . . A DUCK FROM SPACE.

# SO YOU NEED TO SPEAK GROOT

> "I AM GROOT."
> – GROOT, *I AM GROOT*, VOL. 1, #1

The Marvel Universe has more cultures and languages than can be counted—to say nothing of its universal "languages," like justice, mathematics, compassion, and responsibility. It is a rich, endless, and beautiful adventure. A story told by many voices, without any end in sight.

But in all the cosmos, there is one language so beautiful, so musical, so effortlessly poetic that the gods themselves weep at the merest utterance: that of the *Flora colossi* of Planet X. If you plan to travel the universe, memorize these common phrases to show everyone you meet that you come in peace.

| **ENGLISH : GROOT TRANSLATIONS** ||
|---|---|
| "Hello." | "I am Groot." |
| "Excuse me." | "I am Groot." |
| "How much does this cost?" | "I am Groot." |
| "Please." / "Thank you." | "I am Groot." |
| "May I use the bathroom?" | "I am Groot." |
| "Where is the library?" | "I am Groot." |
| "I have injured myself, grievously. I require urgent medical attention." | "I am Groot." |
| "Please forgive the wooden stiffness of my species' larynxes. This has given rise to a common misconception that we all have the same name and are incapable of saying anything else. Allow me to introduce myself. I am the Divine Majesty King Groot the 23rd, Monarch of Planet X, custodian of the branch worlds, ruler of all the shades, frequent saver of the universe, and Guardian of the Galaxy." | "I am Groot." |
| "Goodbye." | "I am Groot." |

**I AM GROOT:**
*I AM GROOT. I AM GROOT!*

# CONCLUSION

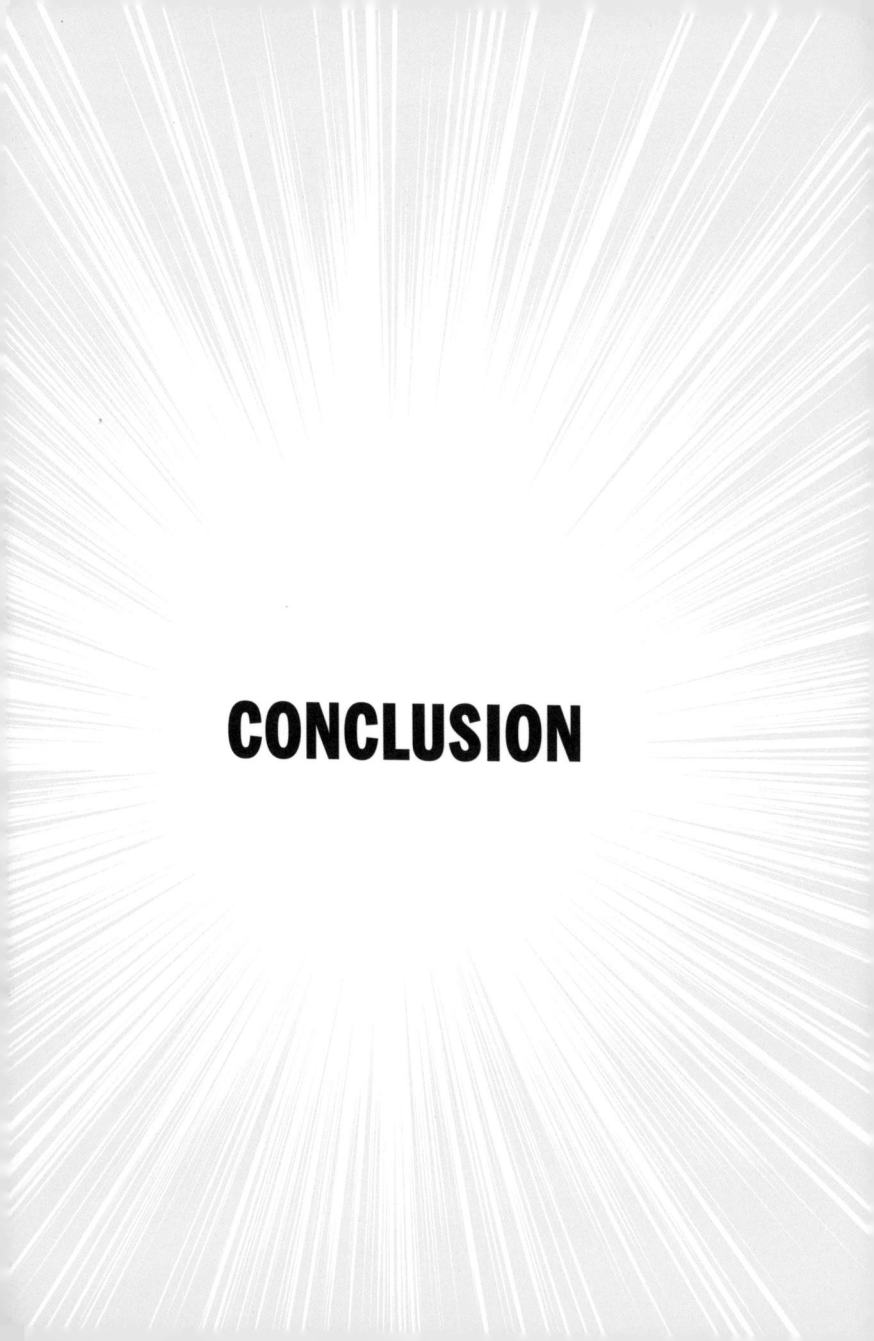

# SO YOU'VE FINISHED THIS BOOK

> "COME WITH ME IF YOU WANT TO BE AWESOME."
> – NOH-VARR, *YOUNG AVENGERS*, VOL. 2, #4

Assuming you didn't just skip to this chapter.

But even if you did, it doesn't preclude greatness. The stories of Marvel heroes are stories without end and are often told out of order. The beginnings are repeated again and again. New adventures are somehow always uncovered in the ever-expanding present. The protectors of this world live many lifetimes and will continue to do so as long as there are lives to save.

And their ranks now include you. You can spot a Skrull, dismantle a Doombot, and hobble a Hydra hive. Your body has been host to enough Phoenix Forces and symbiotes to legally qualify as a short-term rental. You can carry Captain America's shield, wield Thor's hammer, and live up to what they stand for. You can speak enough Groot to ask to use the bathroom—and react with horror when the talking tree behind the counter asks, "What's a bathroom?"

You now carry with you all the training you need to be a hero in the Marvel Universe—and much of the training you'd need to be a villain. With the knowledge contained in this book, you could probably do it with your eyes closed. Especially if you use your radar sense.

Did we—wait, did we teach you how to use radar sense? If you're blinded by radioactive isotopes while pushing an old man clear of the path of an oncoming truck and your other senses are subsequently heightened to a superhuman degree—also resulting in a sixth "radar" sense that allows you to navigate the world in 360 degrees of echolocation—did we walk you through that part?

Well, shoot. Looks like we'll have to do a sequel.

## ACKNOWLEDGMENTS

For Jennifer and Madeline. You are my universe. The author would also like to acknowledge Stan, Jack, Steve, and the Marvel Bullpen (then and now), and Howard the Duck, who is real.

— DK

## ABOUT THE AUTHOR

Daniel Kibblesmith is an Emmy-nominated TV writer for Netflix Animation, HBO, and *The Late Show with Stephen Colbert*, and comics writer for Marvel characters like Loki, Black Panther, Deadpool, and the Amazing Spider-Man, in addition to writing for DC comics and others. He is also the author of the children's book *Princess Dinosaur* and the all-ages humor book *Santa's Husband*. Before that, he worked at *The Onion* and *ClickHole*. He lives in Los Angeles with his beautiful and brilliant wife and daughter.

## ABOUT THE ILLUSTRATOR

Kyle Hilton is a lifelong Marvel devotee and illustrator whose work has appeared in *The New York Times*, *Entertainment Weekly*, *The Wall Street Journal*, and more. As a child, he learned to draw from watching *X-Men: The Animated Series* and redrawing panels from any Spider-Man comic book he could get his hands on. He lives in Jackson, Mississippi, with his wife and daughter.